Testing and Assessment in Occupational and Technical Education

Testing and Assessment in Occupational and Technical Education

Paul A. Bott
California State University, Long Beach

Allyn and Bacon

Boston • London • Toronto • Sydney • Tokyo • Singapore

LB3051 .B641996

Bott, Paul A.

Testing and assessment
in occupational and

Series Editor: Virginia Lanigan
Editorial Assistant: Nihad Farooq
Editorial-Production Administrator: Joe Sweeney
Editorial-Production Service: Walsh Associates
Composition Buyer: Linda Cox
Manufacturing Buyer: Aloka Rathnam
Cover Administrator: Suzanne Harbison

Copyright © 1996 by Allyn & Bacon
A Simon & Schuster Company
Needham Heights, MA 02194

Library of Congress Cataloging-in-Publication Data

Bott, Paul A.
    Testing and Assessment in occupational and technical education /
Paul A. Bott.
        p.   cm.
    ISBN 0-205-16878-7
    1. Educational tests and measurements—Study and teaching.
2. Educational tests and measurements—Design and construction—
Study and teaching.   3. Technical education.   4. Professional
education.   I. Title.
LB3051.B64   1995
371.2'6—dc20   95-1709
                                                                   CIP

Printed in the United States of America

10 9 8 7 6 5 4 3 2 1   00 99 98 97 96 95

Preface

This book was written in response to a keenly felt need for readable, useful, and inexpensive material to use in one of the occupational teacher preparation courses that I teach at California State University, Long Beach. The manuscript has been used in about fifteen different sections of a course in test construction, and the students and their instructor have readily supplied suggestions and criticisms, virtually all of which I have tried to incorporate. It is to those students and to my daughter June whom I dedicate this book: that the students may always fairly and accurately assess their own students, and to June in the hope that she will always be lucky enough to have good teachers.

Contents

▶ 1

Concepts of Testing and Measurement

The measurement and evaluation of student achievement is one of the least understood responsibilities of a teacher. It is not uncommon to observe teachers' evaluating students using criteria and principles that are neither appropriate for measuring student progress nor contributing to learning. It *is* common to observe students being evaluated on the basis of data that are not relevant. It is also common to see teachers administering hastily constructed tests that cover only small parts of the whole learning process. Such processes and tests fly in the face of all that is known about how people learn, and they serve to impede, rather than aid, student growth.

Tests and measurements have been with us in some form or another from the beginning of recorded history. Records from the Chinese—one of the oldest cultures—indicate that they had a highly organized civil service examination system that began before the year 2000 B.C. and was continuously used for nearly two thousand years. This examination system allowed ordinary citizens to become government officials, which of course, opened the door to power and money. Although the Chinese civil service examination was used to determine who would be allowed to be officials, it did not measure the qualities necessary to actually be a good official. This is a problem that is shared with some modern examinations: They do not measure the qualities they purport to measure.

Testing or examinations have always been a part of the educational process. Socrates used oral examinations as the primary component of his teaching strategy. Nearly everyone remembers walking into class at one time or another to hear the teacher say, "Everyone take out a sheet of paper—we're having a quiz." And every year or so throughout the elementary and high school years, students undergo one

1

battery of tests after another. The reputations of schools, school districts, and school personnel are made or broken on the basis of test scores. There are, in fact, documented cases of teachers who have aided students in cheating in order to obtain higher scores (See *Wall Street Journal*, November 2, 1989). Real estate agents often sell houses by touting the test scores of a neighborhood's schools. Homeowners and politicians evaluate schools and neighborhoods on the basis of test scores.

There is also a growing concern for the proper evaluation of employees in the workforce. The use of performance tests plays an important role in such fields as nursing, firefighting, air traffic control, and police work in determining proper job placement and the pace of promotions. The training and development literature is rife with articles on how to conduct performance appraisals, another form of measurement.

As most educators understand it, the concept of evaluation involves a judgment made of the students. When students are "evaluated" in classrooms, teachers are making a determination regarding the totality of their progress and needs, and are placing some value on the degree of progress or ability of the students. The process of collecting data, usually by taking some measurements, is called *assessment*. One of the measuring tools used to make these evaluations is the classroom test. Tests, then, are a part of a process used by teachers to help arrive at some point that indicates the students' growth. At the conclusion of the process, some judgment is usually made when grades or marks are placed on the scale at those evaluation points.

MEASUREMENT

Modern society is probably more "measured" than most people realize. An alarm clock tells us that it is <u>time</u> to get up in the morning. Then we take a 105-<u>degree</u> shower, after which we have a <u>cup</u> of coffee and eat a low-<u>calorie</u> breakfast. Later, it's off to work at 55 <u>miles</u> per <u>hour</u> in our 100-<u>horsepower</u> automobile that will only use one-half <u>gallon</u> of gasoline to get us there in 20 <u>minutes</u> of time. Once at work, we fire up our 66 <u>megahertz</u> personal computer that we are told uses less than a <u>watt-hour</u> of electricity to . . . well, you get the point.

There are few activities in daily life that are not touched by measurement. Some of those measurements are *direct* measures; that is, a scale is placed directly on an object and the units of measurement are counted off, such as when a ruler is used to measure feet and inches. Other measurements are *indirect*, such as when the temperature of a room is taken. Heat cannot be measured directly, but it can be measured indirectly by noting what happens to a thermometer, which is a calibrated glass column filled with alcohol.

The tests that are used to measure student achievement or progress are indirect measures. It is not possible to lay out a person's knowledge or skill level and to use some calibrated scale to measure it directly. Knowledge is intangible—it cannot be touched in a physical sense, so by necessity the tests that teachers use can be nothing more than situations to which students respond. Tests measure or determine the level of psychological constructs, which are nonphysical in form. Achievement is assumed to have occurred when students respond correctly to the situations presented by the teacher in an assignment or a test.

Tests are an important part of the instructional process, and their development should occur early in the process, well before instruction is delivered. Most beginning teachers barely have time to plan the next day's lesson, let alone plan tests before they provide the instruction. But after a year or so of teaching, as teachers redevelop instruction and adapt it to the changing needs of the subject, test development should be a priority on par to instruction delivery. Consider the process shown in Figure 1–1.

Figure 1–1 is an oversimplification of the instructional process, but it is possible to get an idea of how and where tests and other assessments of student progress fit in. Virtually all instruction in occupational education is based on an identification of the job requirements for a specific job. This identification, called the needs assessment, is usually developed in consultation with incumbent employees, supervisors, and others familiar with the job. All aspects of the job—mental, physical, and attitudinal—are included in the assessment.

From the needs assessment, student performance objectives are written. Development of these objectives is covered in a later chapter, so it is sufficient here to say that objectives are statements of what the students will be able to do after instruction to enter satisfactorily, usually at a relatively low level of performance, and advance in employment. To borrow the "garbage-in, garbage-out" adage from computers, it is important to note that if the objectives are garbage, the criteria for achievement will also probably be garbage, so even if students attain the criteria, it will mean little.

When the appropriate level of student performance is set, the next step in the process is to design the methods by which it can be determined if the students actually can perform to the level specified. This is where tests, assignments, and other measures of performance are designed. If the objective calls for cognitive activity such as recalling data or using reference materials, perhaps a paper-and-pencil test will be developed. If manipulation of tools, materials, or instruments is required on the job, the best measure might be some form of performance test. On the other hand, if the objective calls for the student to exhibit particular attitudes, the best method of assessment might involve long-term observation by the teacher or interviews with parents or fellow students.

Only after all of the preceding activities have taken place can the specific methods by which the students will learn, or be assisted in attaining the objectives, be designed and organized. Lesson plans are then created, activities are developed, assignments that focus on the objectives are generated, and the best methods of instruction for each objective are decided. All of this should occur before the teacher does any teaching!

Then the real work begins—the actual in-class or laboratory instruction of students. Teachers lecture, demonstrate, provide a safe classroom, coach students, give

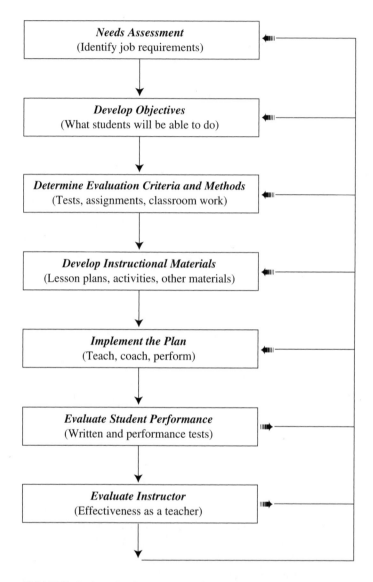

FIGURE 1–1   **The Instructional Process**

assignments, take roll, perform myriad administrative duties, correct homework, and in most cases act as a role model by actually performing the activities of the occupation that they are teaching.

And just when they think it is almost all over, student performance is measured and evaluated. The measurement is taken using those tests, assignments, observations, and classroom work that were planned well in advance of any instruction. In most cases, teachers have to place value on the performance (grade it), and perform yet another administrative duty—give report cards or prepare certificates of competency.

At this point, teachers determine their own effectiveness in the classroom by seeking evaluative feedback from the students, their teaching peers, and their supervisors. This is usually done by comparing the teaching activities to the objectives that were stated at the outset of the process and by obtaining information from the students about their impressions of the effectiveness of the methods used. Peers also will evaluate their colleagues by observing and rating the methods used on some form of rating scale.

You will notice that the process depicted in Figure 1–1 is a closed loop, and never ends. As the process cycles and the effectiveness of a particular assignment, test, or teaching activity is determined, it is possible to go back in the loop and redevelop, reteach, or alter or improve the activity for the next cycle. Just when you thought you were getting off for the summer, you learn that you have to go back and start all over again!

The process depicted in Figure 1–1 is the ideal. In reality, most teachers of occupational subjects are hired on Friday just in time to start teaching on Monday morning. Often, the curriculum, which was designed by a committee, is simply handed to them and they are expected to teach it. On their initial teaching assignment, most occupational teachers come into the process depicted in Figure 1–1 at the second or third step. Only after a few months of teaching do they begin to alter the instruction and the evaluative criteria to reflect what the current workplace and their personal experience dictate. As the workplace and the duties of the job change, the entire cycle is repeated.

At least for the first iteration, then, teachers of occupational subjects are given the objectives and must develop their tests and other measuring devices on the run. When they sit down to develop a test, the first question that needs to be asked concerns the purpose of the test. For example, is the purpose of the test to rank the students in terms of their knowledge levels, or is the purpose to determine which students have mastered the knowledge and skills necessary for success in the subject? In most cases, teachers, advisory committees, state licensing boards, or the subject or occupation itself have identified specific criteria that constitute "acceptable," or passable, performance. The points of reference for these test situations are the information the students must possess and those skills they must be able to demonstrate in order to indicate mastery of the subject. In other words, these things are the criteria that indicate successful performance.

CRITERION-REFERENCED TESTING

One way of deriving meaning from test scores is to make an interpretation of the score with respect to some standard or criterion. A complete student performance objective (which, you will remember from Figure 1–1, was written and used to develop and deliver the instruction) will specify the criteria, and the test will determine when the students have reached the accepted level of performance. Using this method, the passing criteria are based on specific requirements of an occupation, not on the judgment of the teacher. The distribution of a class of students taking such a test and being compared to the criterion standard will appear somewhat as shown in Figure 1–2. Each X in the distribution represents one person taking the examination, and the position of the X represents where his or her score fell. This is called criterion-referenced interpretation, or *criterion-referenced testing.* A criterion-referenced test will determine how well the students' performance at the end of instruction coincides with the performance or behavior called for in the performance objectives. Criterion-referenced tests measure performance in specific courses toward meeting specific objectives; they are not usually purchased from third parties or taken directly from instructor's manuals without careful consideration of the local course objectives. Criterion-referenced testing is also referred to as *mastery testing*, because students who master the specific skills are able to move ahead in the instructional sequence.

Criterion-referenced test results can be and are used with traditional grading systems when different levels of accepted performance are specified in the objectives. For example, the minimum level of passing performance might be specified for a "C" grade, a certain amount of more accomplished performance for a "B" grade, and sustained and excellent performance for an "A" grade. The top two or three scores in Figure 1–2, for instance, might be considered "A," the next two down "B," and the remainder "C." There could be no "D" grade in this scheme, as all those scores below the mastery cut-off would be failing scores.

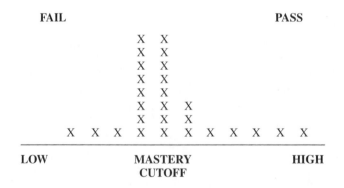

FIGURE 1–2 **Criterion-Referenced Distribution**

NORM-REFERENCED TESTING

Another way of deriving meaning from test scores is to examine the position of the test score in relationship to a *distribution*, or a graphical display of test scores ranked from lowest to highest. The distribution can be derived from a current set of test scores or a set of scores from an earlier date, such as a previous class or a number of previous classes combined. The distribution of test scores used for this purpose is called a *norm*, and the comparison of one class or student to the norm is called norm-referenced interpretation of tests. The tests used are called *norm-referenced tests*. Norm-referenced tests determine individual students' positions within a normative group, such as all tenth-grade students, or all applicants to graduate school. The test items are constructed to discriminate among students as people, rather than to discriminate among several levels of performance within students as individuals. Norm-referenced tests are usually not developed to measure the achievement of any specific objective—they only show the variability of scores of students from the group that they are normed to, for example, all tenth grade students or all applicants to graduate school. Norm-referenced examinations act as sorter devices—they sort students or test takers into various levels. The results of norm-referenced tests are easily transposed to the traditional A-F grading system, although they are not usually used for this purpose. The uniqueness of each classroom makes it nearly impossible for any one standardized or published test to suffice for all uses, so norm-referenced tests have little practical application in daily instruction.

Figure 1–3 is an illustration of a norm-referenced distribution of student scores. Each X represents one person generating the score along the base of the figure. Notice that the distribution has a vague resemblance to the so-called bell curve. More thorough explanations of score distributions may be found in Chapter 12.

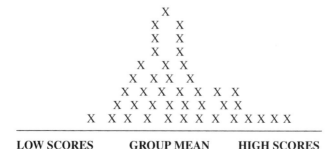

LOW SCORES　　　**GROUP MEAN**　　　**HIGH SCORES**

FIGURE 1–3　**Norm-Referenced Distribution**

TESTING IN THE SCHOOLS

The majority of schools in the United States make use of *standardized*, norm-referenced tests of some kind. Most tests of aptitude, personality, intelligence, and interests are created by publishers, normed with a national group (anywhere from thirty or forty to several thousand in size), and sold throughout the country. Examples of standardized tests include the Iowa Test of Basic Skills, the Scholastic Assessment Test (SAT), the California Basic Educational Skills Test (CBEST), and the Graduate Record Examination (GRE). Few schools or school systems have the staff, the training, or the funds necessary to develop standardized tests for their own use. There are many standardized achievement tests on the market, but most teachers feel that these store-bought tests do not adequately measure their own objectives or the performance objectives for success in the subject area. While standardized tests and their results are useful in some ways (particularly to school administrators and politicians), they are not usually the principal method of measuring achievement in individual classrooms. This job falls to the classroom teacher, and the classroom teacher usually uses a criterion-referenced test, or at least a hybrid of criterion-referenced and norm-referenced items, developed from the specific course objectives.

ARE TESTS ALL THERE IS?

In addition to achievement in the subject area, there are other areas upon which judgments of students are based. Objective measurement is difficult to obtain in areas such as attitude, dependability, cooperation, initiative, appearance, and hygiene, yet these criteria are used to evaluate students. Despite the difficulty, they *are* measurable through the use of written, oral, and performance tests, assignments, and other activities. Each item or behavior that can be measured helps ensure a more equitable and complete evaluation, and teachers should use as many different measurements as pos-

DRABBLE By Kevin Fagan

DRABBLE reprinted by permission of UFS, Inc.

sible. Student learning outcomes, or student mastery of a subject, may be measured and assessed by the quality of written work, by experiments conducted by the students, and by demonstrations of performance. Diagnostic assessments, teacher observation, examinations developed by teachers, and other measures, including standardized tests, are used in the quest for measuring and assessing student performance. Several of these measuring techniques, in addition to classroom tests, will be treated in later chapters.

WHAT'S THIS BOOK ABOUT?

This book is not another erudite exposition of the intricacies of high-powered test and measurement techniques. Instead, the purpose of this text is to provide the classroom teacher with the knowledge of the basic principles and methods of measurement, test construction, and evaluation that can be applied in the classroom and be used to improve learning and instruction. We will be concerned here with the third, sixth, and seventh steps of the instructional process depicted in Figure 1–1. Specific methods that can be used to assess student progress will be described and explained. Particular emphasis will be placed on the several methods of testing for mastery of content and the specific kinds of items used in those tests.

The remainder of the text contains time- and classroom-tested rules for the construction of the most commonly used types of written test items. One chapter is devoted to the development and administration of performance examinations to measure manipulative skills. Another chapter focuses on a number of nontest assessment techniques. Yet another chapter describes how to administer and analyze tests and use test results and other assessment activities to determine grades. A final chapter explores the role of instructional evaluation in the teaching-learning process.

DISCUSSION QUESTIONS

1. What are some of the things that teachers should know about measurement?

2. Can people's knowledge be measured in the same way that inches or feet are measured? Is knowledge measured in the same way that temperature is measured?

3. Think about the standardized tests that you have taken. What were the characteristics of those tests? How did you feel while taking and after you took the tests?

4. When you walked into class and the teacher announced that you were having a test, what were some of the questions that came to mind?

5. Criterion-referenced, or mastery, testing is usually developed to insure that minimum standards are achieved. Proponents of criterion-referenced testing decry the fact that norm-referenced testing often leads to ranking of students and comparing students to each other rather than to job-specific criteria. Can a case be made for ranking of students

in a class? Do you care where your heart surgeon went to school and what her ranking was in her graduating class?

6. As you review your knowledge of tests and testing procedures, what are some of the things that you feel you should learn or would like to learn from this book?

RESOURCES

A Reference List and Selected Bibliography

Anastasi, A. (1988). *Psychological testing*. New York: Macmillan.

Crocker, L., & Algina, J. (1986). *Introduction to classical and modern test theory*. New York: Holt, Rinehart and Winston.

Gronlund, N.E. (1973). *Preparing criterion-referenced tests for classroom instruction*. New York: Macmillan.

Gronlund, N.E. (1981). *Measurement and evaluation in teaching*. New York: Macmillan.

Hynes, W.A. (1994, March). A citizen's remonstrance. *Phi Delta Kappan, 75*, (7), 559–562.

Mitchell, R. (1992). *Testing for learning: How new approaches to evaluation can improve American schools*. New York: Free Press.

Neill, D.M., & Medina, N.J. (1989). Standardized testing: Harmful to educational health. *Phi Delta Kappan, 70*, 688–697.

Ornstein, A.C. (1993, October). Norm-referenced and criterion-referenced tests: An overview. *NAASP Bulletin, 77*, 2839.

Popham, W.J. (1971). *Criterion referenced measurement*. Englewood Cliffs, NJ: Educational Technology Publications.

Popham, W.J. (1987, February). Can high-stakes tests be developed at the local level? *NAASP Bulletin, 71*, 77–84.

Popham, W.J., & Husek, T.R. (1969). Implications of criterion-referenced measurement. *Journal of Educational Measurement, 6*, 1.

Shrock, S.A., & Coscarelli, W.C.C. (1989). *Criterion-referenced test development: Technical and legal guidelines for corporate training*. Reading, MA: Addison-Wesley Publishing Company.

Thorndike, E.L. (1918). The nature, purposes, and general methods of measurements of educational products. In G.M. Whipple (Ed.), *The measurement of educational products*. Seventeenth Yearbook of the National Society for the Study of Education, Part ll. Bloomington, IN: Bloomington Public School Company.

▶ 2

Principles of Learning and Teaching

Before discussing assessment methods and the specifics of creating assignments and tests, it is necessary to review some of the fundamentals of how people learn and how we teach to insure learning. As we will see in the remaining chapters, the very basis of a good test item or classroom assignment is the underlying objective. This chapter contains a review of the three learning domains, their relationship to each other, and techniques for writing the statements of the things students will be expected to master as a result of instruction—student performance objectives.

LEARNING DOMAINS

Educational theorists have identified three major domains in which learning occurs—the *cognitive*, the *affective*, and the *psychomotor*. Each domain is further broken into levels of learning that go from the simple to the complex. Learning occurs in all three domains. To determine learning in the cognitive domain, some form of written or oral test is usually given. Some learning in the affective domain may be determined using written or oral tests, but often it is necessary to observe the students' behavior over a period of time. Learning in the psychomotor domain *must* be determined through the use of a performance (doing) examination.

Cognitive Domain

The cognitive domain deals with knowledge and intellectual learning. A student performance objective requiring a student to calculate the cost of a product would fall into the cognitive domain, as would one that requires a student to describe a process. Behaviors in the cognitive domain usually deal with knowing something, and rarely require any manipulation beyond writing or speaking.

Knowledge
The lowest level of the cognitive domain, *knowledge*, is defined as the remembering of previously learned material. Demonstration of learning to this level generally requires only the recall of material that could range from facts and figures to complete theories. Words used in writing student performance objectives at the knowledge level include:

> define, memorize, name, recall, and repeat

Comprehension
The second level of the cognitive domain is the ability to grasp the meaning of material. This level, *comprehension*, may be demonstrated by translating material from one form to another, such as words to numbers, by explaining or summarizing material, and by predicting consequences or effects of some action. Comprehension might be considered the lowest level of understanding. Verbs used in writing comprehension-level objectives include:

> describe, discuss, explain, express, identify, locate, recognize, report, restate, review, and tell

Application
The ability to use learned material in new and concrete situations (*application*) is the third level of the cognitive domain. Students who have mastered a subject to this level are able to apply rules, concepts, principles, methods, laws, and theories. This is a higher level of understanding than comprehension. Verbs used in student performance objectives written to the application level include:

> apply, calculate, demonstrate, dramatize, employ, illustrate, interpret, operate, practice, schedule, sketch, translate, and use

Analysis
The fourth level of the cognitive domain, *analysis*, refers to the students' ability to break material into its component parts so that its organizational structure may be understood. At this level, students master an understanding of both the content and the structural form of the material. They will be able to recognize unstated assumptions and to distinguish between facts and inferences. Typical verbs used in writing objectives at the analysis level include:

> analyze, compare, contrast, debate, diagram, differentiate, distinguish, examine, inspect, inventory, relate, solve, and question

Synthesis

The fifth level, *synthesis*, refers to the ability to put parts together to form a new whole. Learning outcomes at this level stress creative behaviors such as the formulation of new patterns or structures. Sample verbs for writing student performance objectives at the synthesis level of the cognitive domain include:

> arrange, assemble, collect, compose, construct, create, design, formulate, manage, organize, plan, prepare, propose, reorganize, and set up

Evaluation

Finally, the highest level of the cognitive domain is *evaluation*. As the term implies, students will be able, given specific criteria, to judge the value of material learned for a specific purpose. Learning that occurs to this level is the highest in the cognitive domain, because it contains elements of all the other levels *and* value judgments that are based on clearly defined criteria. The verbs used in objectives written for this level of the cognitive domain reflect the meaning of the term *judgment*, and include:

> appraise, assess, choose, conclude, discriminate, estimate, evaluate, judge, justify, measure, rate, revise, score, select, and value

Remember, the lower the level, the simpler the objective and the lower the level of learning. Most objectives, except at the very beginning of a course or program, should be written to the mid and upper levels. In developing objectives, it is important to remember the level that students must achieve to be successful. The level (criterion) is established in the needs assessment described in Figure 1–1.

Affective Domain

The affective domain deals with attitudes, values, feelings, and emotions. It is nearly impossible to measure directly what a person is feeling, so when writing objectives in the affective domain, we have to seek behaviors that will indicate the feelings or attitudes of the students. For example, a student who (without being prompted) always wears safety glasses, uses the proper guards, and follows safety rules is demonstrating a positive attitude toward safety. A positive attitude toward punctuality or responsibility might be demonstrated by a student who always arrives for class on time and gets right to work.

As in the cognitive domain, the affective domain has been subdivided into levels. It is important to remember that higher-level tasks are not necessarily more difficult. Instead, they demonstrate a deeper understanding and mastery of the subject. Obviously, within the constraints of the classroom, it is desirable for students to learn to as high a level as practical for success.

Receiving
The lowest level in the affective domain is called *receiving*, or *attending*. Student performance objectives written to this level are those that address student behavior ranging from being aware of some stimulus or activity to paying attention. Usually, the students make no response or take no action to what is being taught or what the teacher wishes them to learn. Instead, objectives at this level presume consciousness or awareness only. Verbs used in writing these include:

> attend to, be alert, be aware, be conscious, be sensitive, listen, observe, prefer, and remember

Responding
At the second level of the affective domain, *responding*, students not only receive or attend to stimuli, but they actually respond to them in some fashion. At the lowest point of this level, students participate in an activity at the suggestion of the teacher, but might not do so if given some other options. At the highest point of this level, students might even enjoy what they are doing. Student responses might be measured by using rating scales, or by using their gestures, comments, or laughter as evidence that they are enjoying an activity. Verbs used in writing student performance objectives to the second level of the affective domain include:

> assume, comply, consider, contribute, cooperate, display, engage, enrich, exhibit, explore, extend, look, obey, participate, perform, practice, respond, and volunteer

Valuing
The third, or middle, level of the affective domain is called *valuing*. Student behavior at this level involves placing a value on beliefs or attitudes that have been presented in instruction. Obviously, to value something implies internalization and commitment on the part of the student. Students at this level will spend more time and effort pursuing the value than if they merely accepted it. Verbs used in student performance objectives at the third level of the affective domain include:

> accept, assume, be loyal to, continue to desire, devote, enable, examine, feel, influence, initiate, grow, and participate

Organization
The theme of the fourth level of the affective domain is *organization*, or *organizing the value system*. At this level, students form their value systems by analyzing the relationships of their values and drawing generalizations. An example of behavior at this level is the student who has developed a work ethic and is able to articulate that ethic to other students or potential employers. Verbs used in writing this level of objectives include:

be realistic, crystallize, form judgment, judge, regulate, relate, and weigh

Characterization

The highest level of the affective domain is termed *characterization by a value or value complex,* and it is as difficult to achieve as the title implies. At this level of behavior, a philosophy of life is consistently applied on the basis of a well-thought-out rationale. Needless to say, few people reach such a level of development, especially in classroom situations.

For most subjects and in most classrooms, it is realistic to expect students to develop their affective domain capabilities in the second and third levels. Affective domain development is often confined to such workplace-related areas as professionalism, work ethics, interpersonal relationships, and teamwork.

When measuring performance in the affective domain, it is often necessary for the teacher to rely on checklists of desired behavior and to closely (often indirectly and unobtrusively) observe student behavior.

Psychomotor Domain

The psychomotor domain deals with physical skills such as typing, pounding a nail, manipulating instruments, and walking and chewing gum at the same time. The psychomotor domain has four levels,[*] with the lowest requiring the simple observation of the teacher's actions.

At the higher levels in the psychomotor domain, the student can apply the skills learned in situations unrelated to the ones in which they were learned. The four levels of the psychomotor domain are observation, imitation, practice, and adaptation.

Observation

The lowest level of the psychomotor domain, *observation,* usually is attained when the teacher demonstrates a skill or process in the classroom and explains it to the students as the demonstration progresses. The observation level of the psychomotor domain is similar to the knowledge level of the cognitive domain and the receiving level of the affective domain. In this level, student performance is limited to watching what the teacher does and being able to report on what they have seen. Verbs used in writing student performance objectives to the observation level of the psychomotor domain include:

find, locate, observe, recognize, and sort

---

[*]One theorist has divided the psychomotor domain into five levels, another has identified seven.

Imitation

The second level, *imitation*, requires the student to perform basic "follow the leader" types of activities. For example, the teacher might demonstrate the proper way to perform a given operation and then have the students follow along as a second demonstration is performed. Alternatively, the teacher could provide a job sheet, or list of operations, that the students could take to their workstations and follow in performing the skill. Words used in writing objectives to the second level of the psychomotor domain include:

> build, construct, demonstrate, draw, express, measure, mend, operate, perform, play, run, and use

Practice

The third level of the psychomotor domain, *practice,* implies a higher level of skill development and adaptation than the second level, but the words used in the objectives are the same for the most part. Student behavior in the third level would include working, or practicing, on their own with little supervision. In addition to the verbs used for writing level two objectives, others would include:

> repair, replace, and write

Adaptation

The highest level of the psychomotor domain is called *adaptation.* At this level, the students are able to apply the skills learned at the lower levels to new situations and unfamiliar equipment. For example, students who learned how to use one kind of instrument or tool to the third level would be able to teach themselves how to use a different instrument or tool that performed similar operations. In the field of automechanics, level four or adaptation level proficient mechanics would be able to troubleshoot engines on which they had received no instruction, because they understood the principles and mechanical processes of engines in general and were able to use the tools and equipment necessary to diagnose and repair those engines. The verbs used in writing student performance objectives for the adaptation level of the psychomotor domain include:

> adapt, administer, construct, create, manipulate, plan, produce, promote, and regulate

For most occupations, it will be necessary for students to develop skills at the third and fourth levels of the psychomotor domain in order to be successful in the workplace.

A Note on Words Used

You may have noticed that some of the same words appeared on the three lists, and in some cases they appeared on the same list at different levels. These words either indicate some type of behavior common to two or more of the domains, or a skill that can be achieved at different levels. Always keep in mind the final behavior you wish the students to demonstrate. Think carefully about whether they will be required to use their intellect alone, their feelings or emotions, or whether they will have to perform some physical manipulation. One last list of words follows—a *do not use* list.

appreciate	become	believe	comprehend
enjoy	grasp	know	learn
master	perceive	understand	want

Use of any of these words will lead to a vague and ambiguous student performance objective. Performance has to be described as an observable action. It is difficult to observe or measure "understanding." How, for example, does a teacher know when a student "knows" something? The words listed for the several levels of the three domains are less ambiguous because they provide examples of behavior that are immediately observable. In addition, they are more easily measured through the use of objective evaluation devices such as classroom assignments, tests, or checklists.

Relationship of the Domains

The three domains, while classified separately, are not mutually exclusive. A single objective may require a student to demonstrate learning that has occurred in more than one domain. For example, if the students were required to manufacture a product, they would need to demonstrate psychomotor skills in the manufacturing, cognitive skills in the calculation of needed materials, and affective values in a demonstrated appreciation of quality workmanship. Yet one single psychomotor objective could cover the process: "All students will be able to manufacture a thingamajig."

Most objectives in occupational education are psychomotor, because most of occupational education is skill-oriented. This means that one objective, while on the surface indicating manipulative behavior, will also include behavior in the cognitive and affective domains. After all, in order to perform a skill, we need to *know* a number of things (such as the correct procedure, materials, and processes), we need to appreciate some things (such as quality work or attention to detail), in addition to the physical act of doing what we are doing.

The strength of the students' motivation and the quality of their performances are directly related to their knowing exactly what they have to do and to knowing how well they have performed when they have finished. Performance objectives should not only be shared with the students, they should also be explained fully prior to instruction. If students know where they are going and agree to accompany you, the journey is that much easier and infinitely more enjoyable.

Clear and detailed performance objectives are the first step toward a sound, logical, organized course. Performance objectives allow the teacher to see, well in advance, what instructional strategies will best help students achieve desired behavior and what types of tests are needed to measure that behavior.

LEVELS OF LEARNING

For most purposes, a three-level classification system (applicable to each domain) is adequate and appropriate to the majority of learned activities. These levels are determined by careful study of the tasks of the occupation being taught, or the subject to be mastered. An analysis of the subject or occupation will help determine the degree of manipulative skill needed, the technical knowledge required, the frequency with which specific tasks are performed, the hazards inherent in the tasks, and the extent to which specialization is required.

Level 1—General Knowledge

In the three-level classification of learning, the first level is concerned primarily with the students' ability to follow directions. In order to perform most jobs, it is necessary to remember facts, so instruction is to such a depth that students will recognize an item after their memory is jogged. This level, termed *general knowledge*, requires sufficient knowledge of relationships and necessary associated principles to make information being learned meaningful. Students should have knowledge of the sources from which they might obtain information, and they must develop the ability to follow directions. This level of learning generally requires no manipulation of instruments other than pencils, and few, if any, practical hands-on exercises are used during instructional activities. Instructional activities that will achieve a general knowledge include lecture, supervised research, reading assignments, or some paper-and-pencil problem solving. General knowledge is characterized by:

- Remembering facts
- Recognizing items in response to prompts
- Matching items to establish relationships
- Classifying ideas and generalizations
- Following written and oral directions

Level 2—Working Knowledge

The second level of learning, called *working knowledge*, concerns the depth to which a student successfully recalls something previously learned. The students' abilities are developed to the degree that they can interpret diagrams, drawings, tables, and information in manuals. At this level, the students develop abilities to do such things as translate mathematical verbal material (word problems) into symbolic statements, and vice versa. Required manipulative skills permit performance, usually of limited duration, and are developed to perform basic operations. Working knowledge is characterized by:

- Recalling specific information
- Interpreting diagrams, drawings, tables, symbols, and graphs
- Translating mathematical symbols and verbal statements back and forth
- Performing basic manipulative skills *with supervision*

The development of a working knowledge of a particular subject can be readily achieved by means of conferences, demonstrations, lead-through exercises, and supervised practice.

Level 3—Qualified Knowledge

The top level in the three-level classification system is termed *qualified knowledge*. This level denotes the process by which a student, faced with a new problem or situation, has the ability to recognize common factors and bring new sources and types of information to bear on a new solution. At this level, knowledge and skills are learned in sufficient breadth and depth for the student to transfer earlier learnings to a new set of circumstances, including reflecting on the consequences expected if an action is taken. Manipulative skills are developed whereby performance of a task is efficiently and smoothly executed. Qualified knowledge is characterized by:

- Recognizing common factors that apply to a new problem or situation
- Transferring earlier learnings to the solution of new situations
- Having the ability to analyze or synthesize in order to maintain continual operation of an intricate system and its components
- Weighing the consequences resulting from any action taken
- Planning and performing all specified task-oriented manipulations with a high degree of skill and *without supervision*

To obtain a qualified knowledge, instruction should be geared to develop the students' abilities to apply principles, concepts, and theories to new situations. Level 3 provides a base for transfer of learning, so that when students are employed they can perform productively with a minimum of additional job training or supervision. To accomplish this level of learning requires the inclusion of extensive practical exercises in the instructional program.

It is usually not necessary to learn all things to the highest level in a classroom situation. To attempt to teach all parts of a course to level 3 would be both unrealistic and too time-consuming, even if it was possible. Electronics technicians must know something about the characteristics and kinds of solder (level 1), and they must actually solder connections using manufacturer's specifications (level 2), but they do not need the transfer knowledge about solder that might be needed by a metallurgist or a research worker for a manufacturer of solder. On the other hand, their ability to analyze and trace circuits must be transferable to devices they have never seen (level 3).

Figure 2–1 details the relationship of the three levels of learning to the associated levels of the three domains of learning. A general knowledge level of learning includes the two lowest levels of the cognitive domain, the lowest of the affective domain, and the observation and imitation levels of the psychomotor domain. A working knowledge level of learning (performance with supervision) includes the two middle levels of the cognitive domain, the second two levels of the affective domain, and the practice level of the psychomotor domain. The qualified knowledge, or highest level, includes the highest two levels of the cognitive domain, the highest level of the affective domain, and the adaptation level of the psychomotor domain. At the qualified level, students are able to work on their own, without supervision. For some skills in some occupations, particularly those in healthcare, many of the skills are taught to the qualified knowledge level.

Each instructional activity is classified at the highest level to which the students have to learn or perform in order to be considered successful. Precisely stating the level of learning required will assist teachers in determining what the students will do, the conditions under which it will be done, and the level of minimum acceptable performance. It will also dictate the type of assessment procedure or examination to be used.

	Cognitive Domain	Affective Domain	Psychomotor Domain
General	Knowledge Comprehension	Receiving	Observation Initiation
Working (With Supervision)	Application Analysis	Responding Valuing	Practicing
Qualified (Without Supervision)	Synthesis Evaluation	Organizing Characteristics of the Value Complex	Adaptation

FIGURE 2–1   **A Three-Level Classification System**

PERFORMANCE OBJECTIVES

A great amount of effort goes into determining the content of a course (see Figure 1–1). Once this has been done, these needs analyses are the source for performance objectives. The performance objectives, in turn, reveal a great many factors about what should be taught, in what sequence, how it should be taught, and how it should be tested.

A *performance objective* is a statement of one thing a student is expected to be able to do upon completion of instruction. Student performance objectives are developed from the skills, knowledge, and attitudes revealed as necessary for success in job and task analyses, or for successful mastery of the given subject.

Performance objectives are also commonly known as *behavioral objectives* (because they express behavior changes desired), *observable objectives* (because the changes that occur can be seen), *measurable objectives* (because the change that has occurred can be measured), and *terminal objectives* (because they express a desired end behavior).

By whatever name you call them, meaningful student performance objectives are stated in terms of expected student behavior at the end of the learning period. Students are more likely to be able to perform in the manner desired when these objectives are precisely stated and have been made available to the students prior to and during instruction. Tests and other means of evaluation of the students' progress tell both the instructor and the students to what extent they both have been successful in achieving the student performance objectives.

A student performance objective consists of three basic elements: the *action* or behavior that the students must be capable of performing, the *conditions* under which they are expected to perform, and the *standards* of performance they must reach. By describing each element in detail, an explicit and measurable performance objective is created.

The action or performance element describes an observable end-of-instruction behavior. This is the skill, knowledge, or attitude that the student must be able to demonstrate. It can best be determined by asking, "What will the students be able to do?"

The conditions element, which is derived from the task analysis, should simulate, to the maximum extent possible, actual job conditions. This element should also include the tools, equipment, references, materials, and guides required in the performance of the task, and the supervision and assistance available. These latter items are often called the "givens," because we tell the student in the objective what they will be given to perform the activity described in the first element.

The standards element of a performance objective states how well the student must be able to perform the task. It describes minimum acceptable performance, sets a time limit where applicable, or defines quality and quantity standards for the product or service produced.

One style of objective writing calls for the objective to answer the following question: "Who does what, at (or in) what time, under what conditions, in what amount, and measured by what method?"

The "who" in the question relates to the person or persons who are to perform an activity. For example,

- All students . . .
- Each participant . . .
- The student . . .

The "does what" relates to the activity that is to be known or done as a result of the course, unit, or program (the performance expected), for example,

- . . .will be able to <u>list the various parts of</u> . . .
- . . .will <u>demonstrate</u> a desire to . . .
- . . .will be able to <u>manipulate the controls</u> on . . .
- . . .will <u>describe the preparation</u> . . .
- . . .will <u>prepare the surface</u> . . .
- . . .will <u>inspect five welds</u> . . .
- . . .will <u>remove and replace the</u> . . .

The "time" relates to the specific time when the "does what" will have been learned or done, or the time that is allowed to perform the task on the job. For example,

- At completion of the course . . .
- Within ten minutes...
- By the second semester of the twelfth grade . . .
- In the time alloted for the . . .

The "under what conditions" segment of the question relates to the situation in which the learning will take place, for example,

- In an actual work situation . . .
- In a supervised classroom environment . . .
- With the body submerged under at least ten feet of water . . .
- Given samples of type fonts . . .
- Using only five doodads . . .
- . . .using appropriate reference manuals . . .

The "in what amount" relates to the minimum level to be achieved, or the criteria for success. For example,

- Sixteen of the eighteen muscles . . .
- Three of the four major causes of failure . . .

- At least twice . . .
- Accurate to the nearest whole number . . .
- Five out of eight times . . .
- Within plus or minus two degrees . . .
- So that it meets some specific standard (e.g., licensing) . . .

The "measured by what method" relates to the techniques used for assessing successful completion of the actions required in the objective. Some measuring techniques include:

- As evidenced by 50 of 60 correct answers on a multiple choice examination . . .
- As observed by the teacher . . .
- As indicated by student personnel records . . .
- According to the . . . specifications.

An example of a student performance objective for this chapter might read as follows.

> Upon completion of this unit of instruction, all students (who), when given a list of action verbs denoting performance in their occupations (under what conditions), will be able to write at least ten student performance objectives in each of the three behavioral domains (does what). At least twenty-five (in what amount) of the objectives when compared to a form will contain all answers to the question "Who does what, in what time, under what conditions, in what amount, and measured by what method?" (as measured by).

Calvin and Hobbes   by Bill Watterson

CALVIN AND HOBBES © 1993 & 1994 Watterson. Reprinted with permission of UNIVERSAL PRESS SYNDICATE. All rights reserved.

Good performance objectives are:

1. Relevant—converted directly from a specific task or task element
2. Complete—containing an action statement, conditions, and standards
3. Precise—stated so explicitly that there can be no misunderstanding
4. Measurable—including a means for measuring when and the degree to which the objective has been achieved

SUMMARY

Most human learning can be classified into one of three domains the cognitive, the affective, and the psychomotor. Learning can be further classified into one of three levels: general, working, or qualified. Instruction, classroom assignments, and teacher-made tests should be based on student performance objectives, which, at minimum, will indicate the action the students will be able to complete, the conditions under which they will complete the action, and the standards (criteria) they will meet. The basis for all measurement and evaluation conducted by teachers is the student performance objective. A little work in creating well-stated objectives pays handsome dividends when it is time to measure student performance and evaluate the results.

EXERCISES

1. Classify each of the abbreviated performance objectives found below as: (A) affective domain, (C) cognitive domain, or (P) psychomotor domain. The key indicator of the appropriate domain is the end behavior or action required of the student.

   ___ **a.** Given twenty-five specific situations and two alternative solutions for each, the student will determine which of the two possible solutions to each problem of union unrest is most likely to eliminate the problem.
   ___ **b.** The student will be able to recite the decimal equivalents of common fractional measurements with no more than two errors.
   ___ **c.** The student, within 5 minutes, will be able to thread a film projector properly so that when it is turned on, the film will not flicker.
   ___ **d.** The student will demonstrate an interest in conservation by attending eight out of ten presentations offered during the year by the Outdoors Club.
   ___ **e.** Given descriptions of ten construction projects requiring slabs, the student will calculate the quantity of concrete needed for each within a tolerance of one-quarter cubic yard.

_____ f. The student will demonstrate concern for the democratic principles of free enterprise by articulating at least one principle verbally during an ungraded class discussion.

_____ g. The student will show a growing awareness of health occupations by participating at least twice in health club discussions.

_____ h. The student will be able to transfer bacteria from a culture to a petri dish in a manner that produces properly spread colonies. No contamination is permitted.

_____ i. The student will show interest in industrial occupations by associating the names of at least fifteen job titles with their job tasks out of twenty in an ungraded, optional exercise inventory.

_____ j. After reading an article on small engine performance, the student will be able to summarize the article in no more than 100 words.

_____ k. Using a carbide tip drill, the student will be able to drill a hole of a specified size in tool steel to within .01 of an inch.

_____ l. The student will name the symbols on an electrical schematic drawing with 80 percent accuracy.

_____ m. Given three situations requiring correspondence, the student will compose and type a business letter for each, taking no longer than 20 minutes per letter, with no errors allowed.

_____ n. After watching a rehearsed machining demonstration, the student will be able to criticize in writing at least three safety rules that were violated during the operations.

_____ o. The student will show appreciation for the necessity of sanitation in the foods lab by willingly helping to return clean equipment to its proper place at least three times per week.

_____ p. The students will be able to administer an intramuscular injection using the proper technique.

_____ q. By the end of the second week of instruction, when given standard patterns, all students will be able to compute the amount of fabric needed to within one-half yard of material.

_____ r. All student nurses will demonstrate a positive attitude toward their duties as technologists by willingly seeking out activities that will help polish their skills.

_____ s. The student will be able to read ten different settings on a goniometer within 10 minutes and with no more than plus or minus 2 degrees of error.

_____ t. Given the necessary instruments, the student will be able to measure supination and pronation on a peer to acceptable clinical standards.

2. Select one unit of instruction from the course or program that you teach or are preparing to teach and prepare ten performance objectives for each of the three learning domains. All objectives should be written in such a format that they provide answers to the questions who, does what, under what conditions, in what time, how well, as measured by. Group your objectives according to learning domain, and give an indication of what kind of test you think would be used to determine completion of the objective by the students.

Answers to Exercises

1. C		**11.** P	
2. C		**12.** C	
3. P		**13.** P	
4. A		**14.** C	
5. C		**15.** A	
6. A		**16.** P	
7. A		**17.** C	
8. P		**18.** A	
9. A		**19.** C	
10. C		**20.** P	

RESOURCES

A Reference List and Selected Bibliography

Bloom, B.S. (Ed.). (1956). *Taxonomy of educational objectives. Handbook I: Cognitive domain.* New York: David McKay Company.

Conley, J.C., & Kramer, J.J. (Eds.). (1993). *Tenth mental measurements yearbook* . Lincoln, NE: University of Nebraska Press.

Gagne, R.M., & Briggs, L.J. (1974). *Principles of instructional design.* New York: Holt, Rinehart and Winston.

Girod, G.R. (1973). *Writing and assessing attitudinal objectives.* Columbus, OH: Charles E. Merrill Publishing.

Krathwohl, D.R., Bloom, B.S., & Masia, B.B. (1964). *Taxonomy of educational objectives. Handbook II: Affective domain.* New York: David McKay Company.

Lee, B.N., & Merrill, M.D. (1972). *Writing complete affective objectives: A short course.* Belmont, CA: Wadsworth Publishing.

Lohman, D.F. (1993, October). Learning and the nature of educational measurement. *NAASP Bulletin, 77,* 41–53

Mager, R.F. (1962). *Preparing instructional objectives.* Palo Alto, CA: Fearon Publishers.

Raths, L., Harmin, M., & Simon, S. (1966). *Values and teaching: Working with values in the classroom.* Columbus, OH: Charles E. Merrill Publishing.

Simpson, E.J. (1966). *The classification of objectives. Psychomotor domain.* Urbana, IL: University of Illinois.

▶ 3

The Purposes of Tests in Schools

New teachers, confronted with the myriad responsibilities of the classroom and the limited time within which to perform them, often question the reasons for and the worth of using tests as part of their instructional repertoire. Typical remarks from new occupational teachers often include such comments as "If I want to know whether the students can do something, I will just watch them do it." These teachers—perhaps as a result of their own experiences with tests—view tests as an unnecessary burden added to the teaching process. They lack a clear understanding of the reasons for using tests in the classroom.

The major purpose for using teacher-made tests in the classroom is, and should always be, to improve instruction. One way to determine if instruction is effective (to see if we are doing what we want to do) is to assess how well the students have learned the subject matter of the course. There are several important secondary purposes of tests, including: (1) to determine what areas of the subject may need to be retaught, (2) to determine if students are ready to advance to the next unit of instruction, (3) to assist in reinforcing learning and motivating students, and (4) to provide an objective basis for grades.

The purpose of evaluation, as the word is used in the broadest sense, is to improve the curriculum. The term *evaluation* includes types of measuring instruments such as tests, rating scales, several kinds of classroom assignments, objective observation, and interviews, together with the exercise of judgment. In the following several chapters, the major emphasis is on teacher-made achievement tests, but it must be remembered that there are other means of evaluation that *are* and *should* be used extensively by classroom teachers. The critical point is that any evaluation instrument or technique must be of assistance to the student, the teacher, and the school, or it has little value. This means that unless constructive use is made of the results, there is no value in giving a test or using any other type of measurement. A brief discussion of the uses of tests in schools follows. Ross (1941), who had based his work on that of his teachers Edward Thorndike and William McCall, identified eight uses of tests and measurement in instruction. These purposes, refocused to reflect modern society and educational practices, are still applicable. The purposes stated below are in an order that leads to improved instruction. The priority uses of tests in schools may not necessarily be in the same order.

RETEACHING

Analysis of test results may reveal that the students are weak in specific areas of the subject matter. Instruction time is usually limited, so as a result, special assignments may have to be made to help students catch up if weaknesses are discovered. If the amount of material is small, the entire class might be retaught the relevant material, or out-of-class instruction might be arranged for individuals or small groups.

By studying the results of properly constructed tests, it is easy to obtain a fairly accurate picture of the way students learn. Even novice teachers soon discover what the typical student can be expected to learn. The relative effectiveness and weaknesses of various methods of teaching and teaching materials will be revealed by how well the students have mastered the content taught using that method. Certain parts of courses may need added emphasis and methods of teaching may need to be modified or augmented by other methods. It is important to emphasize the necessity for studying the results of classroom tests in order to make instruction more effective.

Tests can be used to improve instruction, but only if they are carefully made and if the teacher studies the results to determine where improvements might be made. Tests can and should be used as teaching devices. Short daily quizzes are often more important for the teaching that is done in connection with them than for the scores that are made by individual students. Tests and the preparation for them can cause the students to think about the subject and to state their reactions in a manner that is not always possible with other approaches. If such use is made of tests, it might be desirable on occasion to insert deliberately ambiguous items or controversial questions solely for the purpose of motivating student reaction and discussion. Tests with such items should *not* be considered achievement examinations or accurate measures of student mastery, but they can be very useful in a teaching-learning situation. When tests are used in this fashion, it is also a useful technique to give the tests during the first few minutes of the period as one means of getting students motivated and immediately to work.

It is always a sound practice to return the tests or quizzes to the students after the corrections have been made. It seems only fair that the students be allowed to see the extent to which they have been successful, along with the items on which they have not been successful. This practice also provides a good opportunity to reemphasize important points and to reteach as necessary. Such a procedure has to be handled properly, with no place for argument just for the sake of arguing. There will always be students who try to corner the teacher with some arcane or nit-picking reason why they think an answer should be something else, but this is not a valid reason for refusing to allow the students to see their test results as soon as possible. If time can be found for giving tests, time can be found for the students to review their efforts after the tests have been corrected.

The negative side to returning the entire test to the students is that the item pool gets depleted in a few school terms. A solution to this problem is to retain the test papers themselves and use an overhead projector to discuss the reasons for all of the answers with the entire class. The students will have their corrected answer sheets and notes regarding the items they missed and why they missed them, and you will retain your item pool.

When studying test results in an effort to improve instruction, one precaution must always be observed: If the students consistently make high marks on tests, it is not necessarily evidence that the teacher is doing an outstanding job of teaching. Before reaching that conclusion there are several things that must be considered. The success of a teacher can be judged by the accomplishments of the students, but high test scores do not always signify positive achievement. A test may be so easy that even the poorest students do well. In another instance a test may be fairly difficult but will obtain high scores only from those students who take the time and make the effort to memorize the textbook and other learning materials. Such a test may measure memorizing ability or rate of learning with no allowance made for the student's ability to apply the material. Students often concentrate on those things that will enable them to achieve high scores on tests, instead of learning so that they can use and apply the material being taught. Such students learn the testing habits of their teacher and know how to get ready for examinations. This is commonly known as "psyching out the instructor." There are also teachers who "teach the tests." In their instruction, they tend to neglect points that they have not included in the tests, and thus enable students to make high scores that are not a real indication of achievement. This latter practice is more common when teachers are responsible for preparing the students for standardized tests, such as those used in state licensure or some of the college entrance examinations. It is not, however, a sin to teach the test *if* the test is a valid test that accurately measures the course objectives *and* the objectives are accurate indicators of activities and knowledge needed for success in the subject. This point will be discussed further in the next chapter.

ADVANCEMENT

If test results indicate that one or more students are not ready to advance to the next unit of instruction, provision should be made where possible for them to repeat whatever instruction is necessary. This procedure is essential in any case where the unlearned subject matter is requisite for success in mastering the material taught in the succeeding units of instruction.

Tests also often provide an incentive for students to apply themselves to their studies. Think of the times you have made an extra effort in getting ready for a test, and you may then agree that knowledge of an upcoming test is a powerful motive to start studying. To see for yourself if students really do have an interest in test results, just observe their reactions when test papers are returned for review and discussion.

It would be ideal if all students were interested in learning all they possibly could whether or not checks were made on their progress. Unfortunately, this is not the case. A few students will make their best efforts whether or not tests are given, but the majority will work harder if they know that they are to be held accountable for what has been taught. Generally, the teacher who conducts the most thorough program of evaluation gets the greatest amount of work out of the students, and consequently, the greatest amount of learning.

There is a danger in using tests and test results as an incentive for students to apply themselves to work and study. Because they may be focusing on test scores and grades, their efforts may be directed toward passing the test rather than learning the subject matter for its own value. Students who study just to pass a test usually forget the material much faster than those who are interested in learning for learning's sake. A solution to this problem is to give frequent tests that require the students to make application of what they have learned. If the tests have been developed from valid student performance objectives, this practice will lead to true mastery learning.

REINFORCEMENT

One of the principles of learning states that those things often repeated are best remembered. Most of us, for example, can still remember our childhood telephone number but cannot remember one given to us yesterday, because we spent so much time repeating that childhood number in case we got lost or separated from our parents. The more often we see and use something, the greater the chances are that we will remember it. The processes of studying for tests and taking tests require students to remember and apply knowledge "one more time," thereby reinforcing their learning. While there is no guarantee that the students will learn more or better through more practice or repetition of the subject, studying for tests and taking tests will certainly provide the opportunity for learning to take place and for the reinforcement of learning that has already occurred.

GRADES

Most teachers are required to assign a grade to each student. Test results are usually an important component of the formula used in arriving at these marks. When

"My teacher is real tricky. I study hard — she gives me an easy test. I don't study — she gives me a hard test."

© Glenn Bernhardt

criterion-referenced instruction and testing is used, it is necessary to determine which students have reached the minimum standards of performance and which have not. In other instances it is necessary to grade using a five-point scale (A to F). Still other schools use a percentage basis, while some institutions have abolished grades in the traditional sense and have resorted to a more comprehensive statement regarding the students' development and achievement. Whatever method of grading is used, its effectiveness will be closely related to the accuracy of the teacher's evaluation. It is important to keep in mind that students in any class or learning situation learn different amounts. As far as is possible, teachers try to determine the relative amount that each student has learned, compare the amount learned with the stated criteria for success, and then assign grades on the basis of the predetermined standards.

The reliability and usefulness of traditional school grades have been debated for years. It is not the purpose here to argue for or against a particular type of grading system. Instead, given the record, it seems reasonable to expect that we will have school grades of some kind for a long time to come. If these grades are to be meaningful, a first consideration must be the development of more accurate measures of subject mastery. Teachers will have to learn to construct and use tests in such a manner that the resulting grades will be truly indicative of relative achievement. This is a challenge that calls for the best efforts of all teachers.

Teachers usually have to assign course grades to students at specific times. Test scores help make these determinations, but they should *not* be the *sole* basis for grades. Other factors to consider in grading are the results of graded classroom activities, prepared assignments, the rate and degree of improvement achieved and demonstrated by each student, and the attitudes each displays toward the subject. The teacher's personal evaluation of the student as a future member of society or the workforce, although subjective, is a very important factor. A thorough discussion of grading systems may be found in Chapter 14.

ADMINISTRATIVE USES OF TESTS

School administrators are required to use test results to improve the curriculum, but the tests they use are usually nationally normed standardized tests. Such test results often serve as the basis upon which students are classified or classes are grouped.

In the past, tests were used almost entirely for administrative purposes. Teachers used the results as a basis for assigning grades and promoting students from one grade to the next. School administrators examined test scores for the purposes of rating the effectiveness of the teachers in their schools. In certain instances, such as in testing for basic skills, these are still the major reasons for giving tests. The schools where this practice persists as the primary reason for giving tests are usually those that consider their job to be one of pushing students from grade to grade with the hope that by accumulating facts from textbooks the students will become acceptable citizens. The well-prepared educator knows that schooling is much more than dishing out a lot of facts and then testing to see whether the students can just regurgitate them.

Test results are often used by school administrators for justifying expenditures. Boards of education and groups of parents and other citizens are justly interested in the facts that underlie the spending of tax dollars for educational purposes. Humans tend to be creatures of tradition, and it is sometimes difficult to make the public realize the necessity of spending money for a new program or the extension of an old service. Test results are sometimes very helpful in justifying such ventures. For example, subject and other specialists, such as those for reading and special needs, are being employed by more and more schools, a practice that costs money but can easily be justified on the basis of test results obtained before and after the positions are introduced. In other words, test results are often used to hold schools and teachers accountable for their actions and practices.

Another important use of tests and test results is when students transfer from school to school within a system or between systems. With the use of good tests and accurate classroom records, it is possible to minimize the ill effects of transferring from one school to another. Standardized, norm-referenced tests are often used in an effort to get an accurate and complete picture of the students. Valid teacher-made tests and other assessment techniques aid in this endeavor. The administrative uses of tests are closely allied with the importance of adequate guidance.

TESTS FOR GUIDANCE

Guidance, counseling, and vocational guidance are terms that nearly all students are familiar with. Administrators, teachers, students, and parents are all aware of the need for guidance programs that use every possible means to understand individual students better. In order to do this, it is necessary to employ a variety of tests and other measuring instruments. In almost all cases, the tests that counselors use are classified as published standardized tests, not teacher-made.

Specialists in guidance and counseling are usually also specialists in measurement. They are familiar with each of the several types of evaluating instruments used in guidance and counseling and know how to use them, and they are able to interpret the results. A guidance center or counseling office is primarily a testing center where records are kept for all students. Data on their learning abilities, achievements, interests, personal difficulties, and any other significant information are collected, recorded, and interpreted in an effort to obtain a better understanding of the individual. An effective guidance program obtains a large number of portraits of the students in the school, most obtained through the use of some kind of test.

The counseling and guidance function of a school only supplements the work of teachers. Guidance specialists will be the first to agree that the classroom teacher has the most important place in the guidance of individual students. This is another way of saying that teachers must use every means at their disposal to know and understand the students better. Guidance counselors can be useful to teachers in helping to interpret the results of standardized tests and other instruments that provide at least a portion of a picture of the students' potentialities and their limitations. On the other hand, teachers can be of much service to counselors in keeping them informed of student accomplishments, reactions, and difficulties. In either case, the accuracy of the evaluating efforts will help determine the effectiveness of the guidance provided.

CURRICULUM DEVELOPMENT

Well-prepared, valid tests can be very useful in determining the effectiveness of a curriculum. It is sometimes possible to determine the changes that should be made in order to attain the curricular goals by using test results. This approach assumes that tests are devised in terms of the objectives that have been established and that those objectives were established on the basis of and reflect valid job and task analyses. Testing is more than a matter of determining how much subject matter has been assimilated. This is an important point, for it is somewhat at variance in emphasis from the tests that are typically used in classroom teaching.

The usual approach to building a course of study (a curriculum) is to have the instructor, the supervisor, a group of "experts" such as an advisory group, or the teachers alone prepare the course based on the needs of the subject. On the basis of their opinions they decide what is to be taught, when it should be taught, the order of presentation, and how much should be accomplished in a given period of time. This is a very effective approach if all useful data are considered and if the results of the course are continually evaluated. If this or any similar process is followed, it is obvious that tests and other measuring instruments will have to be used in the process. They should help to indicate such things as where changes need to be made, how much should be learned at different levels, and how difficult the subject matter is. In short, the measuring instruments should be devised in such a manner that the real objectives of the course are being measured. This is not easy to do, and it cannot be done entirely by pencil-and-paper tests. Other methods of evaluation such as performance tests, observation, and portfolio assessment may have to be used to provide further information.

TESTS IN RESEARCH

Test results and other evaluating instruments are used for research purposes having to do with administrative problems, guidance, supervision, curriculum, and all other aspects of the school. Educational research is the investigation of problems, so it reaches into virtually every part of the school. In the past, such research was almost exclusively concerned with quantitative measures, and objective tests provided such measures for many types of research problems. Although more qualitative kinds of research are being conducted today, objective tests still play a large role in research. For example, one problem might be to determine the best method of teaching students how to do something. Suppose that three methods were to be investigated: (1) reading about it in a book; (2) seeing and hearing a teacher demonstration; and (3) participating in computer-assisted instruction. Several important steps must be followed in setting up such a research study on a scientific basis, but in this instance we are interested only in the use of tests.

In a simple study, it would first be necessary to have three groups of students who are directly comparable. They must have similar abilities, background, and so on. Before the several teaching methods are tried out there must be a measuring program to determine the similarities and differences within and between the groups. It would be necessary to give intelligence tests and perhaps several types of achievement tests in order to select comparable individuals. This may take more time and effort than measuring the effectiveness of the actual teaching methods being investigated. It would also be necessary to find out ahead of time if any of the students already know how to do what is going to be taught, so a pretest would have to be given. As the teaching progresses, it might be desirable to give a series of tests in order to determine the speed of comprehension, the amount of repetition needed, the permanency of the learning, and so on. This description is not a complete explanation of how such a research project should proceed, but it should illustrate several of the uses of tests in conducting research of this kind. Educational researchers almost have to be specialists in educational measurement.

SUMMARY

The major purpose of any teacher-designed testing program should be the improvement of the instruction and learning that occurs in the classroom. There are several administrative, or nonteaching, purposes of using tests, but the tests used in fulfilling those needs are usually published, standardized tests, not teacher-made tests.

The construction and interpretation of teacher-made tests is not perfect, and probably never will be, but this in no way lessens the importance of using and improving such tests for classroom use. Conscientious efforts on the part of teachers to question the effectiveness of their tests will improve them and add to the quality of the instruction and learning that occurs in their classes. The next chapter contains a discussion of the qualities of good tests. If teachers have a clear understanding of the purposes of tests and the characteristics of good tests, the remainder of this book will become more meaningful and useful.

DISCUSSION QUESTIONS

1. Do the schools in your neighborhood advertise or promote test scores in any way?

2. What are the major uses of tests in your school? What evidence is there that tests and test scores are used primarily to improve instruction?

3. What might be some advantages of (at least temporarily) returning test questions and answer sheets to students?

EXERCISES

1. Visit the guidance or counseling office of your school and select one standardized test from among those used. Explain in your own words:

   a. What is the purpose of the test?
   b. How was it normed (on what population and with what number of individuals)?
   c. How is the test scored and how are the results shared with interested parties?

2. What is the grading policy of your school? Are any specific criteria mandated for inclusion in the grading process? What are they, and what is the rationale for their inclusion?

3. Think of some practical (legal) reasons for giving tests and recording the results for each student. List at least three reasons and describe why they are important.

RESOURCES

A Reference List and Selected Bibliography

Erickson, R.C., & Wentling, T.L. (1976). *Measuring student growth: Techniques and procedures for occupational education.* Boston: Allyn and Bacon.

Mitchell, R. (1992). *Testing for learning: How new approaches to evaluation can improve American schools.* New York: Free Press.

Ross, C.C. (1941). *Measurement in today's schools.* Second Edition. New York: Prentice-Hall.

Wiersma, W., & Jurs, S.G. (1985). *Educational measurement and testing.* Boston: Allyn and Bacon.

► 4

Qualities of Good Tests

Several times in previous chapters reference has been made to "good" tests. Words such as *valid*, *reliable*, and *objective* have been used without explanation in context. This chapter contains a discussion of those terms and a few others that determine the quality of classroom-designed tests. To begin, a good test should be valid, reliable, objective, and practical. Of these criteria, assuming that a test is based on course objectives, validity is the most important.

VALIDITY

The term *validity* is used to indicate the degree to which a test or test item (question) measures what it is supposed to measure. This "measuring what it is supposed to measure" quality is often referred to as *content validity*.

For an entire test to be valid, every item must be related to the stated student performance objective *and* must measure the degree of behavior change sought. Other factors that might affect the validity of test results are the manner in which the test is administered, the physical and emotional condition of the students, and the quality of the instruction. Some tests with long, detailed instructions or written questions are often not valid because they measure the students' ability to read rather than to perform a skill or demonstrate knowledge of the subject. Other tests are not valid because they were written by one teacher for one group of students and were administered by another teacher to another group of students. This is also a problem common to the use of standardized or "purchased" tests used in local classrooms—the tests are not valid for the group and the objectives they are being used for.

Too many teacher-made tests measure memorization rather than application. Suppose a test had been devised to measure the ability of students to apply certain principles in solving problems in their daily living. If the test measured only the students' ability to recall and write down particular facts on paper, it would not be valid because memorizing facts and being able to apply them in real situations are two different behaviors.

Another aspect of validity is that a test designed to measure what students have learned in one course should measure their mastery of that course's material and nothing else. If the test is constructed so that an intelligent student can determine the correct answers without knowing the subject matter, the test measures general intelligence rather than achievement or subject mastery, and is not valid because it does not measure what it is supposed to measure. Or, if the test is written using such a high reading level that poor readers fail because they cannot understand what the test items are asking, it lacks what is referred to as *construct validity* (from the way the test is *constructed*). The test might measure what it is supposed to measure (content validity), but the manner of measuring affects the results.

Other factors that affect the validity of classroom achievement tests include reading ability level, difficulty with memorizing, slow reaction (mental processing) time, limited vocabulary, physical disabilities such as dyslexia, or emotional disabilities. Knowing this, teachers might want to be somewhat skeptical about their test's validity, at least until the tests and test items have been used with several groups of students.

There is no simple formula to follow for determining the validity of a test. A test may be valid for one purpose but not another, or it may measure what it is supposed to measure with one group of students but not with another. For example, a test may be developed that does very well in measuring the achievement of students in a particular subject area, but this does not mean that it will measure equally well the progress of students of a colleague who is teaching in another school. The test might have been an attempt to measure various things that were not even included in the colleague's course of study, the students may be on a different level, or the objectives of the courses may be entirely different. When speaking of the validity of a test, it must be in terms of definite, specified conditions or criteria.

The most rigorous methods of determining the validity of a test compare the test with some predetermined criterion of validity, much in the same way that manufacturers of scales and other measuring instruments compare their products with physical specimens from the National Institute of Standards and Technology. Another way is to compare the results of the new test with the results of one that is known to be highly valid. This form of validity is called *concurrent validity*. Needless to say, typical classroom teachers only rarely have the time, training, and resources to use this latter method to determine the validity of their examinations.

The most commonly used method of determining the content validity of teacher-made tests is somewhat subjective in nature. In a properly designed test, certain specific objectives that have been established and are agreed upon for the course are (or should be) measured. They describe what the teacher is trying to measure, just as a standard unit of length describes a much simpler property in exact terms. On the basis of these clearly stated objectives the test can be submitted to several competent people (such as other teachers or advisory group members) who are thoroughly familiar with the content of the field being tested. After studying the various parts of the test in terms of measuring the behavior or performance specified in the objectives, they give their opinion on the validity of the test by telling whether they think it will measure what it is supposed to measure. As a result, various changes, corrections, or additions can be made, and the test can be said to have content validity. When compared with physical measurements such as length and weight, this practice appears crude and subjective, but if carried out thoroughly and conscientiously, it will result in a test much more valid than those ordinarily used in the classroom. In fact, as will be shown in later chapters, the teacher's own, unaided critical inspection of test items and complete tests will result in improved validity.

One other aspect of validity should be considered in constructing any teacher-made test, namely, the validity of individual items. The validity of the total test will be dependent upon how well each item does what it is supposed to do. In many respects, it is more useful and desirable to give first attention to the validity of the individual items than to the validity of the test as a whole. Such reasoning would assume that, if the various items are in themselves valid, the total test should therefore be valid. For practical purposes, this is true, although the relationship between validity of individual test items and validity of the total test is more than a process of simple addition. The process of determining the validity of individual items is usually carried out as the items are constructed simply by answering one question: Will this item really measure what it is supposed to measure?

The most important feature of any examination is its validity. The factors of reliability, objectivity, discrimination, comprehensiveness, and practicality might be discussed as a part of validity, since they affect validity, but they will be treated under separate headings below.

RELIABILITY

The term *reliability* is used to express the degree to which a test gives consistent results each time it is administered, provided the classes to which the test is given are of the same ability level and that the test is given each time under similar conditions, including a like amount of instruction. Reliability is difficult to guarantee, especially the first time the test is given, but several practices help. First, the test should be long enough to provide thorough coverage of the subject matter. Short tests increase the chance that only familiar items are being covered. Second, elements that will increase the chance of guessing correctly should be eliminated. (This will be covered later under each of the types of test items.) To help guarantee reliability when giving performance tests, for example, it is important to make certain that all materials and equipment used in the test are in approximately the same condition.

A reliable test is an accurate and consistent test—its results can be trusted. A test is said to be high in reliability if it measures in exactly the same manner each time it is administered and if the factors that affect the test scores affect them to the same extent every time the test is given. In other words, a highly reliable test should yield essentially the same score when administered twice to the same student, provided, of course, that no learning occurs while the test is being taken the first time or no learning or forgetting takes place between testings. These are difficult assumptions to make.

The reliability of tests is closely connected to their validity. If a test is valid, it must be reliable. That is, if a test measures effectively what it is supposed to measure, then presumably it does this accurately and consistently. On the other side of the token, it must be remembered that a test may be highly reliable and still not be valid: It consistently measures the same phenomenon, but that phenomenon may not the one that was intended to be measured.

An oral thermometer, for example, is a measuring instrument for determining body temperature. Like a test, it must be valid and reliable to be of any use. If a particular thermometer measures the body temperature accurately and consistently, we could say that it is both valid and reliable because it measures accurately what it is supposed to measure. We can depend upon it. It has to be reliable before it can measure effectively what it is supposed to measure. Most people would agree that the thermometer is highly reliable, yet it could not be used in the coronary care unit to measure blood pressure, because it would not measure what it is supposed to measure. In this instance, the thermometer would be reliable but not valid. In the same fashion that thermometers are not valid measurement tools for determining blood pressure, true-false tests are not valid measurement tools for determining a student's ability to perform manipulative operations.

A test developed by a teacher may be valid for one class in that teacher's subject. In order to be valid it has to be reliable. This same test might also be highly reliable if given several times to a colleague's class in another subject. But no matter how reliable it might be in measuring the abilities of the first teacher's students, it would not be valid in the second teacher's class because it would not measure achievement in that subject. To repeat, a test must be reliable in order to be valid, but a test can be highly reliable and still not be valid.

It was stated earlier that achievement tests often measure attributes other than achievement, such as reading ability and general intelligence. This characteristic is also common to teacher-made tests. These factors—reading ability and intelligence—are considered to be constant, and must be excluded if the validity is to be trusted. Reliability, however, is often affected by factors that vary each time a test is given. Remember that if a test is reliable, you should get approximately the same score if you take the test a second time. Suppose that on a given test the various items are subjective in nature (open to interpretation) and the teacher has difficulty in scoring them, maybe even giving credit for a certain item on one student's examination and marking the same thing wrong on another. In another instance a student may feel fine the first time a test is taken and get a high score; at the second test, the student may be coming down with a cold and not care about anything, particularly the score on a test. One time the room may be quiet; the next time it may be noisy. Perhaps the test is too short, or the students guess differently each time. These are all examples of variable factors that affect the reliability of a test. As can be imagined, there are about as many variable factors as there are people taking the test.

One method for determining reliability is to prepare two equivalent forms of the test and administer them to the same group under the same conditions, with little or no time in between. This method of determining reliability is called the *Equivalent Forms Method*. Forms 1 and 2 of the test would measure the same objectives but would use different test items. After giving the tests, the scores would be compared to determine the reliability. If the test is high in reliability, the person who scored high on form 1 would also score high on form 2. The low scorer on one would be low on the other. A coefficient of correlation (a statistical relationship) would be obtained to indicate the extent of reliability.

While the above method might be satisfactory for determining reliability, most teachers do not have the time or the energy to prepare two equivalent forms of the same test, so another approach is to give the same test a second time. This method, called the *Test-Retest Method*, presumes that enough time has gone by so that the students will have forgotten the details of the test. It also assumes that the achievement level is about the same. When using the Test-Retest Method, the reliability is again determined by obtaining the coefficient of correlation between the two sets of results on the test.

Another method of determining reliability is to divide the test into two parts, with the first part containing all of the odd items (1, 3, 5, and so on), and the second part containing all of the even items (2, 4, 6, and so on), and determine the correlation between the two halves of the same test. This method is called the *Split-Half Method*. Since each form is only half as long as the complete test, a formula is used to indicate what the reliability would be if the length were increased. When applied, this correction formula—called the Spearman-Brown Formula—establishes the reliability for the entire test. The Spearman-Brown formula is as follows:

$$\text{Entire test reliability} \;=\; \frac{2\,(\text{Reliability on } \tfrac{1}{2} \text{ test})}{1 + (\text{Reliability on } \tfrac{1}{2} \text{ test})}$$

The length of the test, the clarity and objectivity of the items, the simplicity of the directions, and the objectivity of scoring are all factors that influence reliability. By concentrating on these considerations, the reliability of teacher-made tests can be improved. This means that the reliability of a test can generally be raised by increasing the length. The more responses required of the student, the more reliable the measurement of achievement. The smaller the chances of guessing the correct answer to each item in the test, the greater the reliability. Clear and concise directions also increase the reliability of the test. Confusing directions and complicated and ambiguous items decrease the reliability. These points will be discussed in detail later in the chapters on constructing specific types of test items.

OBJECTIVITY

The term objectivity refers to (1) the degree to which a test can be scored without bias or the personal opinion of the scorer affecting the grades, and (2) the interpretation of individual test items by the test taker. Objectivity is an important factor that affects both the validity and reliability of an examination.

Scoring Bias

The personal judgment of the individual who scores or corrects the test should not be a factor that affects the score. Several people should be able to score the test and get the exact same results. After the key has been made, there should be no question as to whether an item is right or wrong or partly right or partly wrong.

Essay tests, as usually constructed and scored, register poorly when measured by this standard. People who are competent to judge rarely agree on the score that should be recorded for a given essay-test paper because they do not have a common objective basis for marking. Similar discrepancies result when several teachers are asked to "grade" projects or drawings on a subjective basis.

When scoring essay test papers or projects, teachers often notice that students are making higher marks than usual. As a result, they begin to grade "harder." That is, they begin to take off more points for errors. The reverse of this also happens when the students seem to be making low scores. Naturally, such a system is neither objective nor fair to the students and cannot be tolerated in an assessment program. In order to gauge the subjectivity of the essay-type of test, several competent teachers of the same subject have to be selected and each one independently scores the same test paper covering materials that all of them teach. Even then, there will be considerable variation in the scores recorded for the single test paper unless some kind of guideline, or rubric, is followed. If the same teachers score the same test papers again one week later, the difference between the first and second set of scores is likely to be large enough to be significant.

A simple experiment with some fellow teachers or fellow students might help erase any doubts about this. Give the fellow teachers or students an essay-type test or completed project, and have each person independently score it with no other instructions than to give a letter grade or percentage mark. After the marks are in, carry the experiment one step further and ask each person to indicate how they arrived at the score given, or why they scored it as they did. There will undoubtedly be a variety of answers.

This discussion is not meant to serve as a condemnation of essay questions. Nor should it be assumed that such items should be eliminated from tests. On the contrary, the fault lies in the construction and scoring of such items and is not a fault of the items themselves. When carefully constructed, an essay-type item measures the ability of students to organize and express their thoughts. Specific points on the construction and use of essay items are presented in Chapter 10.

Student Interpretation

The second aspect of objectivity, equally important but more subtle and therefore more frequently neglected, has to do with the students' interpretation of the items in the test. Well-constructed test items should lend themselves to one, and only one, interpretation by students who know or who have mastered the material involved. In other words, a given test item should mean essentially the same thing to different students who know the point in question. This goal is difficult to attain. Students are prone to read into test items meanings that were never intended by the test maker (and the students will usually try to gain clarification in the middle of the test by waving their arms or loudly asking a question). In spite of how good a test item may appear at the start, there may be some students who interpret it wrongly. Obviously, this will affect the validity.

Stop for a moment and recall various tests that you have taken. How many times have you thought, "Just what in the bleep is the teacher looking for?" In such instances you may have known well the subject matter being tested but may still have been unable to determine the answer that was "wanted." The item may have been ambiguous; it may have been inconsistent; the grammar may have been misleading; or there may have been some other subjective element that made it difficult to interpret the item. People who have taken many tests (like all of those who have gone through a teacher preparation program) have experienced this difficulty and should therefore strive to locate and remove or revise such items in the tests they make or use.

In constructing and using tests, the teacher must be constantly aware of student reactions and interpretations, even taking the time to "debrief" students after a test. Following this practice will make it much easier to detect and correct weaknesses of this type and to learn to avoid ambiguous items. Items that are clearly understood by the students will be the end product. As a result, the validity and reliability of the tests will be increased. This point will be discussed further in the chapters that cover specific types of test items.

FUNKY WINKERBEAN TOM BATIUK

Reprinted with special permission of North American Syndicate

Validity, reliability, and objectivity as related to the construction of teacher-made tests have been discussed to this point. While each has been treated separately, it should be obvious by now that they are closely related and interdependent—there is no fine line of demarcation between them. But that is not the end of the matter; there are still other factors that enter into the relationship of validity and reliability.

DISCRIMINATION

A test discriminates when it picks out the students who have mastered the material and those who have not. The ability of a test to discriminate is essential if the test is to be used reliably to determine which students have mastered the subject, for ranking students on the basis of achievement, or for assigning grades. Three things will be true of a test that meets this standard:

1. There will be a wide range of scores when the test is administered to students who have actually mastered amounts that are significantly different. If the full range of mastery is to be measured, scores are likely to vary from the lowest to the highest possible scores. In most classes and for most subject-matter fields, scores will vary from near the highest possible score to a score that is around one-half of the total number of points on the test.

2. The test will include items at all levels of difficulty. That is, the items will vary uniformly in difficulty from the most difficult one, which will be answered correctly only by the best students, to an item so easy that practically all the students will answer it correctly. (This is important if students are being ranked.)

3. Each item will discriminate between students who are high and those who are low in mastery or achievement. Each item will be missed more frequently by poor students than by good students. If the good students are just as likely to miss an item as the poor students, the item does not measure in a positive direction. Poor, or poorly prepared, students will often answer correctly certain items that the best students miss consistently. Such items discriminate negatively. An examination of these items usually reveals that they are ambiguous or technically weak in other respects. They are not objective from the students' point of view and therefore do not discriminate positively. The good students are able to detect the second, hidden, unintended meaning, and as a result they often make a response different from the one intended by the teacher. In such instances the good students mark the item wrong, and the poor students select the right answer. Again, this is negative discrimination.

The discriminating power of a test is increased by concentrating on and improving each item in the test. After a test has been administered, a simple item analysis can be made that will help to indicate the relative difficulty of each item and, of greater importance, the extent to which each discriminates between students who have mastered the subject and those who have not. This technique is thoroughly treated in Chapter 12.

COMPREHENSIVENESS

Comprehensiveness refers to the test being long enough and containing an appropriate number and type of items to do the job.

If you were asked to give an opinion on the merits of a particular restaurant, you would want to do more than walk into the restaurant, take a look at it, and make your statement. You would probably want to taste some of the food too. At the same time it wouldn't be necessary to eat everything on the menu before passing judgment. A sample item from each section of the menu would do if you could be sure it was typical of the entire menu. If there were three different sections on the menu, you would want to sample all three before making a statement. If your sample only contained one item from one section of the menu, you might have an idea about the rest of the food, but you could not be sure about the other sections without sampling them also. The interest here is not in how you determine whether the sample is good or poor, but concerns only the importance of getting an adequate sample upon which to base your decision. It is not necessary to eat all of the menu selections, but it is necessary for the sample to include all the sections.

In constructing teacher-made tests it is equally important to sample all objectives and phases of instruction that are supposed to be covered by the test. It is not necessary and it would not be practical to test every point that is taught in the course, even on "final" examinations. The questions, then, are how long should a test be? How much of a sampling should it include? How comprehensive should it be?

A test should be comprehensive enough to be valid. It should include enough points so that it completely measures what it is supposed to measure. This is an easy statement to make but somewhat more difficult to put into practice. There is no specific formula that indicates when a test meets the criterion of comprehensiveness—it is a matter of the test maker's judgment. For the classroom teacher, the best advice is to consider this question carefully: Is this test comprehensive enough to measure accurately and thoroughly what I expect it to measure?

PRACTICABILITY

Practicability describes the extent to which a test is usable. This includes the test's readability, its ease of administration and scoring, and the time, material, money, and personnel required. Tests that are poorly duplicated or that make excessive demands on time and personnel are not practical.

Consideration must be given to the features of the test that make it readily administered and scored. The test should be designed so that a minimum of student time will be consumed in answering each item. The test items should also be constructed in such a manner that they can be scored quickly and efficiently.

These characteristics of good tests would seem to be logical and understandable without further elaboration at this point. Later chapters on the actual construction of a test and specific types of items will contain various suggestions that will make for ease of administration and scoring.

SUMMARY

Tests (and other classroom assignments) must meet certain requirements before much faith can be placed in their use. The first requirement is that the test or assignment must be able to do what is expected of it—it must have content validity. Validity is an inclusive term. The reliability, objectivity, discrimination, comprehensiveness, and practicality of a test all may cause the validity to be altered. Reliability denotes accuracy or consistency. A valid test must be reliable, but it is possible for a test to be reliable and still not be valid. The reliability of a test may be improved by eliminating the variable factors that affect the total test score such as guessing, the subjectivity of the items, and the length of the test.

Objectivity is closely related to both validity and reliability. An objective test item is one where there is no question regarding how it should be scored. At the same time, such an item will have a clear meaning to all the students who take the test and know the subject matter being tested. A test may have low validity because it is not reliable or because it is not objective.

Discrimination refers to the ability of a total test or individual test item to differentiate effectively between the students who know the material and those who do not. An indication of discriminating power can be obtained by making a simple item analysis. A test must be comprehensive enough to be valid. It must sample all the objectives and instructional processes that are being measured by the test. Finally, a good test will be practical in that it will be easy to administer and easy to score.

DISCUSSION QUESTIONS

1. What is the difference between a subjective and an objective test?

2. What are the advantages and disadvantages of using objective tests?

3. Imagine that you are in the process of constructing a single test item. What can you do to check on or improve the validity of the item?

4. How is the term *reliability* related to the statistical term *correlation*?

5. What method(s) can you use to determine the reliability of your tests? What would be the most effective method? Why?

6. What relationship is there between the comprehensiveness of a test and the objectives being measured?

7. How can a test be reliable but not valid? Give an example from a test that is or could be used in teaching your occupation.

EXERCISES

1. In your own words and in a manner that will be useful to you in the classroom:

   a. Explain the meaning of validity.
   b. Discuss at least three elements that can affect a test's validity.
   c. Describe how you will determine whether your tests are valid.

   Your answer should be written in paragraph form of sufficient length to respond to each area, a-c.

2. In your own words, describe the process you would use to determine whether your tests were reliable tests. Consider such things as the time available, the expense, and the personnel needed.

RESOURCES

A Reference List and Selected Bibliography

Bloom, B.S., Hastings, J.T., & Madaus, G.F. (1971). *Measuring educational achievement*. New York: McGraw-Hill.

Cronbach, L.J. (1988). Five perspectives on validity argument. In H. Wainer & H.I. Braun (Eds.), *Test validity*. Hillsdale, NJ: Erlbaum.

Diederich, P. (1960). *Shortcut statistics for teacher-made tests*. Princeton, NJ: Educational Testing Service.

Feldt, L.S., & Brennan, R.L. (1989). Reliability. In R.L. Linn (Ed.), *Educational measurement*, pp. 105–146. New York: Macmillan.

Gronlund. N.E. (1965). *Measurement and evaluation in teaching*. New York: Macmillan.

Hills, J.R. (1976). *Measurement and evaluation in the classroom*. Columbus, OH: Charles E. Merrill Publishing.

Marshal, J.C., & Hales, L.W. (1971). *Classroom test construction*. Reading, MA: Addison-Wesley Publishing Co.

Messick, S. (1989). Validity. In R.L. Linn (Ed.), *Educational measurement*, pp. 13–104. New York: Macmillan.

▶ 5

Teacher-Made Tests

Evaluation, as we learned in Chapter 1, is an integral part of the learning process—a lesson or a unit of instruction is not complete until the extent of the students' learning has been determined and documented. If the objectives have been properly specified, whenever learning takes place, the result should be a definable, observable, and measurable change in behavior. The process of evaluation is concerned with defining, observing, measuring, *and* judging this behavior. Teachers usually observe students' reactions during the presentation of a lesson and periodically ask them questions to check their understanding. These activities are a form of evaluation, and they indicate that evaluation occurs at many points in teaching and learning—not just at the end.

Evaluation is a common process, something we engage in every day. We judge the merits of the weather, the fit of our clothes, and how our car's engine performs. These efforts at evaluation are all attempts to determine the worth of something and are usually informal and unconscious. Teachers also make informal evaluations in the school situation when, for example, they listen to a piece of equipment and decide that it is running poorly, or when they walk into a classroom for the first time and sense intuitively that it will be a good class or a poor one.

The teacher's evaluation of student learning and performance cannot be an informal process. Administrative demands and the students' right to know the criteria upon which their grades are based require that evaluation in the classroom be a formal, objective process of measurement. One of the ways this determination of student achievement is often accomplished is through the use of teacher-made tests.

Tests are but one of the ways teachers use evaluation in education. Teachers evaluate themselves and each other in order to determine their effectiveness, and entire programs are evaluated with respect to their cost, the rate of placement of graduates in jobs or higher education, and their overall effectiveness.

Much of this book deals with teacher-made tests for determining the students' level of mastery of the subject. The reasons for conducting different types of evaluation and some of the techniques for performing them are discussed in this chapter.

The evaluation process usually includes the use of written tests that are prepared by the teacher specifically to determine the students' cognitive gain. Another kind of test, the *performance test*, is prepared to determine exactly how well the students can perform the activities detailed in the course objectives. Performance tests are also called *authentic assessments* because the students must perform a task that is authentic, or actually used when practicing the subject in "real" life. Whatever their type, tests vary in length and importance, and they may be administered in formal or informal manners.

Teachers are responsible for developing individual test items; preparing, administering, and scoring the examinations; and evaluating the results. Each of these responsibilities is examined in the subsequent paragraphs. Later chapters will provide instructions for the preparation of specific types of test items and their evaluation.

GENERAL PRINCIPLES

The construction of satisfactory tests (that is, those that are valid and reliable) is one of the most difficult duties that a teacher has to perform. It is a rare teacher who can prepare a good test in a short time on the first try. Some general principles for constructing teacher-made tests follow. The rules presented in this chapter apply to all teacher-made tests. These rules are an amplification of Figure 1–1, which illustrates the instructional process. Rules that apply to specific types of test items follow in subsequent chapters.

Relate Test Items to Objectives

Each school or school system has a group of broad-based objectives commonly referred to as citizenship or general objectives that it wishes to achieve for all students. The subject matter itself is the source of the objectives for individual classes. For occupational education subjects, the requirements for survival and success in the workplace will determine the objectives. In order to create effective tests that relate to the objectives of the course and the institution, the teacher must first formulate careful statements of educational objectives in terms of expected student behavior and indicate in which learning domain(s) the behavior would be classified. See Chapter 2 for a review of objectives construction.

Then, for each objective, a situation or situations should be listed in which the students could be expected to demonstrate the behavior described in the objective. This step will also dictate the best teaching technique to use for each objective.

The third step is to determine which of those situations lend themselves to examination in the classroom or educational environment. A general rule to guide in this process is that those objectives that require behavior only in the cognitive domain might best be measured by some form of oral or written test; those in the affective domain require some kind of observation of behavior; and those in the psychomotor domain will require use of a performance examination.

The final step in insuring that the test is related to the objectives is to devise the means (test items and test environments) to determine the level to which the objective is met. This is the mastery cutoff point described in the discussion in Chapter 1 on criterion-referenced tests: the lowest level of performance acceptable for demonstrating mastery.

Plan the Test

Once the educational objectives have been specified, the actual planning of the test may begin. Many teachers find it expedient to write down potential items to be included in tests each day as teaching progresses. This practice assures that important items in the course are included when the draft of the test is prepared. It also permits the potential test items to sit for a while (so teachers are not so attached to them that they cannot critically review them) before they are included in the test. When

" NUMBER THREE IS MR. HUGO, OUR SEVENTH GRADE TEACHER—THE ONE WHOSE EXAM CONTAINED QUESTIONS NOT COVERED IN THE ASSIGNED READING."

© Harley Schwadron

planning, adequate provision must be made for examining or evaluating all the important outcomes of instruction. It is absolutely essential that the school philosophy (articulated in the citizenship objectives) and the course objectives be available to and accepted by the teacher from the start of instruction.

The test or tests used should reflect the same proportion of emphasis that particular behaviors or matters of content have in the course. In other words, two-thirds of the test should not cover information or behavior that only one-third of the course was spent on. For occupational teachers, the job or task analysis that is used to develop objectives will provide this balance. Ultimately, any test created should reflect the emphasis of the teacher throughout the period of instruction covered by the test. A good indicator of this emphasis is the amount of time devoted to topical divisions of a course. If three hours of a fifteen-hour unit of instruction (20 percent) is spent on a particular topic, approximately 20 percent of the test should be on the same points. Be advised though, that the amount of time spent on a given topic is at best an indicator of the *number* of items to be included—not the *type* of items. The type of items used will depend on the nature of the objective being measured. This will be explained further in Chapter 12.

When planning the test, attention must be given to such factors as the time available for testing, the equipment needed for duplicating the test, and the cost of the materials.

Prepare the Test

Once all items have been prepared for a test, the next step is the preparation of the test form. A helpful practice is to prepare a draft of the actual test several days in advance of the time it is needed. This will allow an unhurried perusal of the test in time to make corrections or amendments prior to duplication and administration. Instructions specific to the preparation of individual types of items and the directions to accompany them are included in later chapters.

A general rule for test construction is to include more than one type of item, especially in long tests. A number of test item types will make the test more interesting to the students as well as assuring that appropriate items are used to measure behavior for specific objectives. A long test, such as a comprehensive final examination, might contain two to four forms of objective questions.

When tests are being prepared for the purpose of ranking students (norm-referenced tests), the test items should range from the very easy to the very difficult for the group being measured. The item difficulty should range from some items so easy that the least able students can get 50 percent of them correct to others so difficult that the most able students get only 50 percent correct. Note that this does *not* say that some students should only get 50 percent of the items correct on the exam. With maximum discrimination, the difficulty of the entire test would be such that an "average" student would make about 50 percent of the possible score. While this might make an ideal test for discrimination purposes, it is not likely to do much for the morale of the students, and as such is not recommended for typical classroom applications. Chapter 12 contains instructions on how to determine the difficulty level of test items, a process that cannot be carried out prior to test administration. Teacher judgment is the only criteria the first time around.

When preparing the preliminary draft of a test, it is a good idea to include more items than will be needed in the final form. This permits culling items that might be weak or not needed to produce a balanced test. After some time has elapsed, critically read the preliminary draft. Better yet, have another teacher read the draft to look for items that cover material of doubtful importance, are not clearly stated, or for which there may be doubt as to the correct answer. Particular attention should be paid to the wording of items to avoid ambiguity.

Test items should be written so that the content, rather than the form, of the item determines the answer. Telltale words or phrases give clues to the students and lead to the answer, even for those students who do not know the content. These telltale words or phrases, called *specific determiners*, are especially common in true-false items. The form of the item should neither pose an obstacle for the students nor provide obvious clues. The items should be worded in such a way that the whole content of the question functions in determining the answer, rather than only a part of it. In other words, include only enough words to make the item complete.

Place all items of a particular type, such as true-false, together in the test. Items designed to measure a particular objective should be placed together, unless, of course, they are of a different type. Arranging items this way not only facilitates the scoring of the test, but it helps the students by keeping them in the mindset imposed by a particular form of question.

The items of the test should be arranged in order of difficulty, with the easiest items at the beginning and the hardest at the end. The rationale for placing the easiest items first is that the morale of the students taking the test is given an immediate boost by getting off to a good, successful start. Before administering a test for the first time, it is difficult to get more than a rough estimate of the true difficulty order of the test items unless several other knowledgeable people provide a pooled judgment. Fortunately, an experienced teacher's judgment regarding the difficulty of the items will have considerable validity. After administration and analysis, test items can be placed in a more exact order of difficulty in later revisions.

A regular sequence in the pattern of responses should be avoided. The pattern should be random in order to prevent the student from figuring it out. Many people have a "favorite" response letter that they use for the correct answer when constructing tests, so be aware of this. Computerized test construction programs will usually place the answers in a random order, but this is not always a regular feature.

The last two steps in preparation for giving the test are to write clear, concise, and complete instructions for taking the test and to prepare an answer sheet for the students. In the instructions, the students should be told how and where to mark the answers, the time alloted for taking the test, the weight of each item and the total for the test, and whether or not guessing is encouraged.

Try Out the Test

After the test has been prepared, it is time for it to be given a trial in actual use. The first time the test is given, it should be given under as normal conditions as possible—in the regular classroom at a regularly scheduled time. A little extra time should be allotted the first time, just to make sure that all students have sufficient time to answer all questions. Adopt a simple scoring scheme (one point per response), particularly for the first time the test is given. Finally, prepare answer keys and scoring rules before the test is given. If partial credit will be given for incomplete answers, share this information with the students in the test instructions.

Evaluate the Test

After the examination has been given and scored, the results should be interpreted from two perspectives: first, in terms of the quality of the test itself, and second, in terms of the quality of the students' responses. Sharing the responses with the students was discussed in Chapter 3 in the "reteaching" section of using test items in the instructional process. Chapter 12 contains more complete details of how to interpret and analyze test results.

Figure 5–1 is a graphic indication of the process of developing a test from course objectives. Notice that the evaluation step allows the test maker to re-cycle to the appropriate point in the process to improve the items and the entire test.

THE ETHICS OF TESTING

A final but most important element of this chapter is the issue of the ethics of testing. This topic is usually brought up in relation to standardized or norm-referenced tests, or professionally developed tests that are prepared for sale and dissemination to large audiences, but the issue deserves treatment in a discussion of teacher-made tests. In the mid-1980s, the American Educational Research Association, the National Council on Measurement in Education, and the American Psychological Association formed a Joint Committee on Testing Practices, which in 1988 produced the Code of Fair Testing Practices in Education. While the code specifically indicates that it is not intended for tests developed by teachers for classroom use, the principles listed in the code, for the most part, follow the rules for constructing tests that have been delineated in this chapter and those in following chapters. The code presents standards in the areas of developing and selecting tests, interpreting scores, fairness, and informing test takers. Further, it addresses issues of importance to both test developers and test users. Unlike the rules for constructing tests found in most texts, the code addresses ethical and moral issues of test construction and administration. For example, the code raises the issue of whether tests, in some instances, are the best ways of obtaining the information sought. The code admonishes test users to provide timely

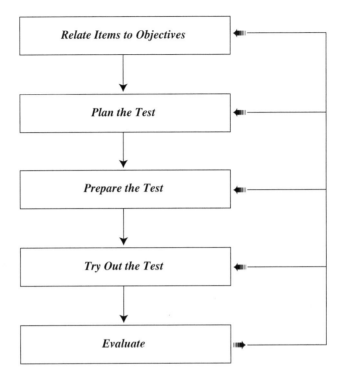

FIGURE 5–1 **Developing the Test**

information to test takers regarding their scores, and to provide the information in a fashion that is easily understood to the students (and their guardians). The code also indicates that test developers and users should strive to develop and use tests that are fair to individuals of different cultures, gender, and handicapping conditions. Single copies of the code may be obtained free of charge from the National Council on Measurement in Education, 1230 Seventeenth Street, NW, Washington, DC 20036. Include a business-size stamped, self-addressed envelope when requesting copies of the code.

SUMMARY

A comprehensive program of testing is an important part of every teaching-learning situation. Testing highlights the successes of the instructional process and its short-comings. Ultimately, testing and test results are used to improve the process.

A good testing program will compare all elements of instruction and student learning with the objectives of the program or course. Techniques and instruments will be developed to measure how well objectives are being met. Teacher-made tests are the primary methods used to determine students' level of mastery of the subject, and they are one of the key elements in the formulas used for determining grades.

There are a number of ethical issues in the development and administration of tests that teachers should be aware of, including determining whether tests are the best way to gather the needed information, issues of gender and cultural differences, and the return of test results to the test takers in a timely fashion.

DISCUSSION QUESTIONS

1. Why is it necessary to give some attention to the manner in which a test is to be scored?
2. Knowing what you now know, why do you suppose is it so difficult to measure a person's attitude accurately and reliably?
3. Is grading the same as evaluation? Why?
4. You give an examination and the majority or all of the students do poorly. What are the things that you need to explore?
5. What are some of the ethical issues involved in the development and administration of tests?
6. Why is it necessary to consider the language ability or cultural background of test takers in your classes?
7. In addition to the "right to know," are there any educational reasons (principles of learning) why test results should be shared with test takers in a timely fashion?

EXERCISES

1. Is a so-called objective test strictly objective? Describe the characteristics of an objective test and explain why some tests that are touted as being objective really are not. Think of some of the tests that you have taken that were not really objective.

RESOURCES

A Reference List and Selected Bibliography

Airasion, P.W., & Madaus, G. F. (1972). Criterion-referenced testing in the classroom. *Measurement in education*, 3 (4), 1–8.

Boyd, J.L., Jr., & Shimberg, B. (1971). *Handbook of performance testing.* Princeton, NJ: Educational Testing Service.

Erickson, R.C., & Wentling, T.L. (1976). *Measuring student growth: Techniques and procedures for occupational education.* Boston: Allyn and Bacon.

Gronlund, N.E. (1965). *Measurement and evaluation in teaching.* New York: Macmillan.

Hill, P., Harvey, J., & Praskac, A. (1994). *Pandora's box: Accountability and performance standards in vocational education.* Berkeley, CA: National Center for Research in Vocational Education, University of California at Berkeley.

Hills, J.R. (1976). *Measurement and evaluation in the classroom.* Columbus, OH: Charles E. Merrill Publishing.

Hopkins, K.D., Stanley, J.C., & Hopkins, B.R. (1990). *Educational and psychological measurement and evaluation.* Seventh Edition. Englewood Cliffs, NJ: Prentice-Hall.

Joint Committee on Testing Practices (1988). Code of fair testing practices in education. Washington, DC: American Psychological Association.

Mager, R.F. (1973). *Measuring instructional intent.* Belmont, CA: Fearon Publishers.

Payne, D.A. (1968). *The specification and measurement of learning outcomes.* Waltham, MA: Blaisdell Publishing Co.

Saville-Troike, M. (1991). *Teaching and testing for academic achievement: The role of language development.* Washington, DC: National Clearinghouse for Bilingual Education.

Tyler, R.W. (1973, Spring). Assessing educational achievement in the affective domain. Special report by the National Council on Measurement in Education, *4.* (3).

Wiersma, W., & Jurs, S.G. (1985). *Educational measurement and testing.* Boston: Allyn and Bacon.

Williams, R., & Miller, H.G. (1973). Grading students: A failure to communicate. *Clearing House, 47* (6), pp. 332–337.

▶ 6

Constructing True-False Items

True-false tests are one of five basic kinds of written tests used to determine student achievement in the cognitive domain. True-false items consist of a series of statements that the students are asked to judge as being either true or false. This chapter discusses the uses and misuses of true-false items, describes several different types of true-false items, and gives samples of their construction.

ADVANTAGES OF TRUE-FALSE ITEMS

The true-false item is used by teachers at all levels of education and is therefore known to the students. This is an advantage because students know how to answer the item, but there is also a negative aspect to consider. Students quickly learn the weaknesses inherent in many true-false items and are able to obtain high scores by noting the grammatical construction, the choice of words, or other clues. True-false items are relatively easy to construct, so they are used extensively. But the advantage of ease of construction is offset by the doubtful quality of many true-false items.

A wide range of subject matter can be sampled with the true-false item. Average students are able to answer between three and five true-false items a minute, so a large number can be included in a single test. Naturally, the rate of answering will vary with the type of student and the type of material being tested.

Perhaps the most important but least used application of the true-false test is as an instructional platform to promote interest and introduce points for discussion. Because the true-false item is relatively easy to construct and can be answered in a short time, it is a valuable and economic way to give short daily tests (quizzes) that may be used to motivate the students for a new assignment, to review a previous lesson, to determine content to be retaught, or to introduce controversial points for class discussion. Unfortunately, few teachers take advantage of this use.

True-false items can be constructed either as simple factual questions or as questions that require reasoning and discrimination. The latter type of question is more difficult to prepare than simple statements. Modified true-false items (described later in this chapter) lend themselves more readily to the more difficult approach.

When there are only two choices governing a particular point it is especially practical to use true-false items. Multiple-choice items cannot be used effectively with such content since there are only two plausible answers, and, as you will see in Chapter 7, multiple-choice questions require at least four choices.

One type of true-false item, called *cluster true-false*, can be used to check several points concerning a particular concept, principle, or mechanical unit. When well constructed, cluster true-false items tend to more accurately reveal the student's complete understanding.

Modified true-false items can be designed to correct many of the weaknesses noted below. They can be designed to require the student to exercise judgment and use knowledge in situations that call for understanding rather than mere memorization. The modified true-false form should be substituted for the simple true-false item whenever possible.

A final advantage is that true-false tests can usually be administered and scored quickly and in an objective manner, even when the more exotic variations are used. The benefit of this to students and teachers alike should be readily apparent.

LIMITATIONS OF TRUE-FALSE ITEMS

Major limitations or disadvantages of the simple true-false items are that they have doubtful value for measuring achievement and that they encourage guessing because there is an equal chance that either answer will be correct. While mathematical formulas are sometimes applied to the test results to counteract this weakness, many students will guess anyway. In many true-false tests, items can be answered correctly without any knowledge of the subject matter involved because of grammatical clues.

It is difficult to construct items that are either completely true or completely false without making the correct response obvious. It is also difficult to avoid ambiguous questions, unimportant details, and irrelevant clues. Many true-false items are copied directly from textbooks—another common weakness.

True-false tests are likely to be low in reliability unless they include a large number of items. This disadvantage limits the advantage of using them as instructional tests. Minor details often get as much credit as significant points in true-false tests, and they are difficult to construct if the material is in any way controversial.

Numerous variations and modifications have been developed in an effort to capitalize on the advantages and to correct certain weaknesses inherent in true-false

"Boy! A few more like that and I'll be ready for Gamblers Anonymous."

First published Phi Delta Kappan 11/93

items. Samples of several varieties of true-false items are presented on the next few pages. Still other adaptations can be created by the resourceful test maker.

REGULAR, OR SIMPLE, TRUE-FALSE

The unmodified regular true-false item usually consists of a simple statement that may be either true or false. Students are required to indicate whether the statement is true or false. This type of item has been used extensively, and in many instances indiscriminately. Several samples, shown in Figures 6–1 through 6–8, illustrate methods that are used in constructing the regular true-false item and for indicating responses. Each variation of the simple true-false item is found in a separate box with a figure number. Sample directions to the student are included for each variation of item. The variation in the examples shown in Figures 6–1 through 6–8 generally is in the manner in which students respond to, or answer the item. Most teachers adopt the answer method that they or their students are most comfortable with and stick to it on all tests. Most of the samples shown indicate that the answer is to be written directly on the test sheet. It is a simple matter to change the directions to indicate that the answer should be placed on a separate sheet, and this is in fact recommended in most instances.

Directions: Some of the following statements are true and some are false. If the statement is true place a plus (+) in the blank space at the left. If the statement is false place zero (0) in the space. The first item is answered as an example.

   _+_   x. Holding open houses is a good public relations tactic for use with the general community.

   ___   1. It is normal for students to resist learning in a classroom.

   ___   2. It is important that learning be accompanied or followed by a feeling of pleasure.

FIGURE 6–1   **True-False Using Plus and Zero for Answers**

Directions: Listed below are a number of statements. Some are true and some are false. If the statement is true, draw a circle around the "T" at the left of the statement. If the statement is false, draw a circle around the "F." The first item is answered as an example.

(T)   F   x. The systolic pressure is the numerator of a blood pressure reading.

T   F   1. The brachial artery is the artery used to palpate for a blood pressure.

T   F   2. The adult male's blood pressure may be slightly higher than the adult female's.

T   F   3. The waiting period between taking blood pressures on the same patient and the same arm is 2 minutes.

FIGURE 6–2   **Drawing Circles around the Answer**

Directions: A series of questions is listed below. Each of them can be answered by "yes" or "no." Draw a circle around the correct answer at the left of the question.

Yes   No   1. Must learning be goal-centered to be successful?

Yes   No   2. Should teachers make it a practice to use lavish praise to encourage students?

Yes   No   3. Is hearing the most important sense used in learning?

FIGURE 6–3   **Using Yes and No Responses**

Directions: Several true and false statements are listed below. You are to check (✔) only those items that are false. Do nothing if the statement is true.

( ) 1. Approximately 85% of what people learn is absorbed through their eyes.
( ) 2. Effective learning arises from memorizing isolated facts or mastering bits of operations.

FIGURE 6–4   **Answering Only False Items**

Directions: Listed below are a number of statements. Some are true and some are false. If the statement is true, draw a circle around the "T" at the left of the statement. If the statement is false, draw a circle around the "F." DO NOT GUESS. Your score for this section will be found by subtracting the number wrong from the number right. The first item is answered as an example.

Ⓣ F 1. To remember, learners must actively participate in or experience what they are expected to learn.

T F 2. If the material to be learned is a manipulative skill, actual practice of the operation will be necessary before it has been learned.

FIGURE 6–5   **Correction for Guessing**

Directions: A series of words listed below. Some are spelled correctly. Some are misspelled. If the word is spelled correctly, place a plus (+) in the blank space preceding the word. If the word is misspelled, place a zero (0) in the blank space. DO NOT GUESS. Each wrong answer will subtract two points. Each omitted answer will subtract one point. The first word "femoral" is spelled correctly so a plus (+) has been placed in the blank space as an example.

__+__ x. femoral   _____ 5. carrotid
_____ 1. popliteal   _____ 6. dorselis
_____ 2. antaspetic   _____ 7. sooture
_____ 3. fourceps   _____ 8. orel
_____ 4. aneroid

FIGURE 6–6   **Written Spelling Test**

Directions: Listed below are various common formulas. Some are stated correctly. Some are incorrect. If the formula is stated correctly place a "C" in the blank space at the left. If the formula is incorrect place an "I" in the blank space. The first formula is incorrect. Therefore an "I" is placed in the blank space.

   _I_   x. $CS = 3.14 \times D \times RPM / 120$

   ___   1. $E = I / R$

   ___   2. $1 = E / R$

   ___   3. $Area = Length \times Width$

FIGURE 6–7   **Mathematical Formulas**

Directions: All of the following statements concern one topic. If the statement is true, draw a circle around the "T" at the left of the statement. If the statement is false, draw a circle around the "F."

T   F   1. There are 12 points in a pica.

T   F   2. Type sizes are measured in picas.

T   F   3. A pica is one-sixth of an inch.

T   F   4. Leading is measured in points.

T   F   5. An en space is one-half the width of an em space.

FIGURE 6–8   **True-False Items Related to Each Other**

CLUSTER TRUE-FALSE

Cluster true-false items are very similar to the regular, or simple, type. They usually consist of an incomplete statement followed by several phrases or clauses, each of which will complete the statement. Students are required to indicate those phrases or clauses that form true and those that form false statements. Sometimes the cluster of statements will be related to a drawing or photograph reproduced just before the items. This type of item, sometimes called a multiple-response item, is not used extensively, but in many cases is more effective than the simple true-false item. In such instances students may be required to pick out only those items that are true or those that are false. This begins to approach the multiple-choice type of item. Sample cluster-type true-false items are shown in Figures 6–9 through 6–12. Directions to the student are included for each sample. Figure 6–9 contains sample instructions for use with a separate answer sheet. The benefits of such a practice will be described in a later chapter.

Directions: Each of the incomplete statements below is followed by several items, each of which will complete the statement and make it either true of false. A separate sheet is provided for your answers. Make your decision with regard to each statement and mark the appropriate letter on your answer sheet. DO NOT make any marks on the examination paper.

A true-false test is used:

1. for the purpose of assigning students a grade.
2. to test both skill and knowledge.
3. as a teaching aid.
4. to determine students' ability to recall facts.

A true-false test should avoid;

5. negative statements.
6. statements that stress only one idea.
7. ambiguous words.
8. specific determiners.

FIGURE 6–9   **Cluster True-False Items**

Directions: The incomplete statements below are followed by several phrases, each of which completes the statement and makes it true or false. If the completed statement is true, draw a circle around the "T" before the item. If false, draw a circle around the "F."

Effective CPR on an adult patient is affected by:

T   F   1. maintaining the patient's airway.
T   F   2. ventilating the patient once every 7 seconds.
T   F   3. performing compressions on the lower half of the sternum.
T   F   4. compressing the sternum $2^{1}/_{2}$ to 3 inches.
T   F   5. performing compressions at the rate of 90 to 100 per minute.
T   F   6. delivering 2 ventilations for every 15 compressions.

FIGURE 6–10   **Cluster True-False Item—Different Answer Mode**

Directions: The following questions pertain to the diagram at the top of the set of questions. Each question can be answered by "Yes" or "No." If the correct answer is "Yes," draw a circle around that word at the left of the item. If the correct answer is "No," circle that word.

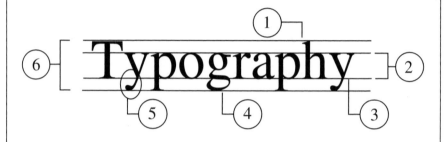

Yes No 1. The number 1 represents the descender part of the letter.

Yes No 2. The number 2 illustrates the x-height of the lower case x in a type face.

Yes No 3. To determine the point size of a letter, you would need the properties of numbers 1, 2, and 3.

Yes No 4. Number 5 indicates the serif of the letter.

Yes No 5. The number 6 illustrates the cap height of the letter.

FIGURE 6–11 **Multiple Response Based on a Diagram**

MODIFIED TRUE-FALSE

There are many variations and modifications of true-false test items. These modifications correct certain of the weaknesses and have much greater testing value than the regular, or simple, items. Modified items are usually more difficult to construct, and unless carefully done, often lead to tests that measure reading ability more than they measure subject knowledge. Clear and concise directions to the students become especially important when using modified items.

Directions: The diagram below is a detail for a single-story concrete-slab foundation. Five materials required to meet the design criteria as specified by the *Uniform Building Code* have been called out. If the description of the item is correct, draw a circle around the letter "T" next to the appropriate number on your answer sheet. If the description is incorrect, draw a circle around the letter "F" next to the appropriate letter on your answer sheet.

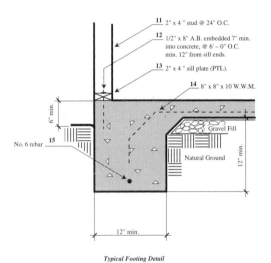

Typical Footing Detail

11. $2'' \times 4'' \times$ studs @ 24" O.C. are used to erect the exterior walls.

12. $\frac{1}{2}'' \times 8''$ A.B. embedded 7" minimum into concrete @ $6'-0''$ O.C. and 12" min. from sill ends is used to secure the sill plate to the foundation.

13. $2'' \times 4''$ sill plate (PTL).

14. $8'' \times 8'' \times 10$ W.W.M. is used to reinforce the concrete slab.

15. Number 6 rebar is used to reinforce the footing.

FIGURE 6–12 **Multiple Response Based on a Diagram—Second Example**

One variation of true-false items is to require the student to mark the items that are true, but to modify the false items either by (1) crossing out the word that makes the statement false, or (2) identifying the word that makes the statement false and listing another word that would make it true. Another variation requires the student to justify the response, whether true or false. Still another modification has the student choose the correct word from a list of words. Whenever possible, the variations and modified forms should be substituted for simple true-false items. Figures 6–13

Directions: Some of the following statements are true and some are false. If the statement is true, draw a circle around the "T" at the left and <u>do no more.</u> if the statement is false, draw a circle around the "F" and do two more things:

1. In blank "A," insert the word that makes the statement false.
2. In blank "B," insert the word that would make it true.

DO NOT USE WORDS THAT ARE UNDERLINED. The first item is answered as an example.

T Ⓕ 1. For most subject fields, a range between the high and the low grades of approximately one-quarter the total number of possible points is an indication of good discrimination.

    A. _____1/4_____   B. _____1/2_____

T F 2. When a teacher wonders if the instruction has been weak in certain areas, the location of any weak points can be determined through the use of a general achievement test.

    A. _____   B. _____

T F 3. It is called a <u>crisis</u> when a fever drops abruptly within a 36-hour period..

    A. _____   B. _____

T F 4. The most critical part of the cost approach is estimating depreciation.

    A. _____   B. _____

T F 5. Filenames are always 8 characters or less and allow for no space before or after the extension.

    A. _____   B. _____

FIGURE 6–13 **Modified True-False Items**

through 6–19 contain samples of modified true-false items. As with the preceding samples, directions to the students are provided.

Sometimes when using items of the type shown in Figure 6–13, students will be able to change the meaning of the statements by changing words that you did not have in mind. In such cases, it is necessary to underline the words that the students are *not* to use and to instruct them accordingly. It can save considerable paper to use a separate answer sheet with items of this type, since the test sheets can be reused if they are not written on.

Compound true-false items, such as those shown in Figures 6–14 through 6–16, are very difficult to construct, and even more difficult for students to answer. The

---

Directions: Some of the following statements are true, some are false. If a statement is true, draw a circle around the "T" at the left and do no more. If the statement is false, draw a circle around the "F" <u>and underline</u> the one word that makes it false. The first item is answered as an example.

T   (F)   x.   <u>Picas</u> are used to calculate point size.

T   F   1.   Typesetting arithmetic is based on a unique system of measurement, the basic units of which are the pica and the inch.

T   F   2.   Picas are used to calculate the width and depth of the type.

T   F   3.   Negative letter spacing is called tracking.

T   F   4.   Set width is a fixed value assigned to each character of each word.

T   F   5.   Justified copy is flush on the left and ragged on the right.

FIGURE 6–14   **Underlining the Word That Makes the Statement False**

case can be made that compound items test reading ability more than they test subject matter knowledge. They are valuable items to use to test complex reasoning skills, but it would probably be easier for the test maker to construct an essay-type item, as described in Chapter 10.

    The items shown in Figure 6–17 would also be considered compound true-false

---

Directions: Some of the following statements are true, some are false. If the statement is true, draw a circle around the "T" at the left <u>and explain</u> why it is in the blank spaces below the item. If the statement is false, draw a circle around the "F" at the left <u>and explain</u> why it is false. The first item is answered as an example.

T   (F)   x.   Beach sand may be used in concrete when quarried sand is not available. Explanation: <u>(Beach sand should never be used in concrete. The salt in the sand interacts negatively with the cement and the reinforcing material.)</u>

T   F   1.   The command ^QC would be the best to use when trying to get from the beginning of a large file to a place three pages from the end. Explanation: _____

T   F   2.   The amount of room between the developer sleeve and the drum determines copy clarity. Explanation: _____

FIGURE 6–15   **Explain Why a Statement Is True or False**

Directions: In the following statements certain conclusions are drawn that may or may not be true. If you think that statement is true, draw a circle around the "T" at the left. If you think it is false, draw a circle around the "F." THEN, draw a circle around one or more of the reasons (A, B, C, etc.) that support the judgment you have made. In some cases there will be only one correct reason, in others more than one. (The first item is answered as an example.)

T (F)
A   B   C   D   (E)   1. All teachers, regardless of the subject they teach, should have the same preparation.

        A. It is too complicated to have different program requirements for different teachers.

        B. Some teachers will develop inferiority complexes if they do not all have the same education.

        C. Teacher training should take account of different subject's requirements.

        D. If teachers are paid the same, they should have equal preparation.

        E. All students deserve to have equally well-prepared teachers.

T   F
A   B   C   D   E   2. When a lot of woodwork is used in room, the walls should be covered with materials of different textures.

        A. The woodwork will serve as a focal point in a room.

        B. This would be a means of introducing color at structural points.

        C. The room will appear to be too "busy."

        D. Woodwork should not be contrasted with walls.

T   F
A   B   C   D   E   3. When researching careers, you should gather information about one specific career.

        A. Public libraries have information about many careers.

        B. Friends or parents are the best source in determining which job is best for you.

        C. Talk directly with workers in various careers.

        D. You can learn about different careers by working part-time.

FIGURE 6–16   **Compound True-False Items**

Directions: If the following items are true, draw a circle around the "T" and do no more. If the item is false, draw a circle around the "F" and explain in the blank why it is false.

T   F   1. Intelligence is the sum of an individual's many different abilities to learn, and it represents potential capacities.
          Explanation: _____
          _____

T   F   2. Intelligence is believed to be determined largely by environmental factors.
          Explanation: _____
          _____

FIGURE 6–17   **Explain Why Statements Are False**

items because they require the students not only make a judgment regarding the veracity of the statement, but also to explain from memory or using reason why they are incorrect. The controlled-correction items shown in Figure 6–18 do not determine learning to as high a level as those in Figure 6–17 because the extra words listed allow the students to *recognize* correct answers (a low level in the cognitive domain) in the context in which they are commonly used.

The example shown in Figure 6–19 requires the student to distinguish between true and false statements and to then determine the word that makes the statement false

Directions: The true and false statements below refer to knowledge and practices used in dental assisting. If the numbered statement is true, draw a circle around the "T" at the start of the item and do no more. If the statement is false, circle the "F" and also underline the correct word in the list just below the item. The first item is answered as an example.

T   Ⓕ   x. There are 22 permanent teeth.
              (18, 28, 32, 38)
T   F   1. The deciduous teeth replace the primary dentition.
              (permanent, canine, molar, wisdom)
T   F   2. Dental impressions are usually made from a form of rubber.
              (spirit gum, resin, plastic, malleable paste)
T   F   3. Cuspids are also commonly referred to as canines.
              (incisors, mandibulars, molars, anteriors)

FIGURE 6–18   **Controlled-Correction Type**

Directions: Some of the following statements are true, some are false. If the statement is true, draw a circle around the "T" preceding the item and do no more. If the statement is false, circle the "F" and do two things.

1. Underline the word that makes the statement false.
2. From the list below select the word that would make the item true and place the letter preceding that word in the blank space before the item. The first item is answered as an example.

A. cam shaft	F. overlap	K. timing
B. solid lifter	G. pushrod	L. train
C. valve lash	H. ports	M. seat
D. rocker arms	I. valve	N. exhaust
E. hydraulic	J. lobes	O. head

T　(F)　x.　_N_　The intake valve controls the flow of burned gases from the cylinder.

T　F　1.　___　The valve train opens and closes the ports of an engine.

T　F　2.　___　The dome is the large casting bolted to the top of the engine.

FIGURE 6–19　**Underline False Word and Make Statement True**

and replace it with a word from a list provided that will make it true. These items measure to a higher level of the cognitive domain than do regular true-false items, but they are much more difficult to construct properly.

CONSTRUCTING TRUE-FALSE ITEMS

Several rules should be followed when constructing true-false items in order to minimize their limitations. Ross (1941) first compiled these rules, but in somewhat different language. The rules have been time- and research-tested and have since been repeated in virtually every text on test construction.

Be Aware of an Answer Pattern

Make approximately half of the items true and half false. If you are in the habit of having significantly more true statements than false statements, the students soon become aware of this, and whenever they are in doubt about a certain item, the "smart thing" is to mark it true. The students then have a better than 50 percent chance of guessing the correct response. There should be no set pattern in distributing the true and false items throughout the test. In other words, make sure that the students will not be able to mark an item false simply because a certain number of true statements precede it and therefore it is time for a different response. Avoid this problem by randomly distributing items.

Use Simple Methods of Response

Make the method of indicating responses as simple as possible. Do not make the student write out "true" or "false" or "yes" or "no, since this just takes up time. Do not employ a system in which there is any question as to whether the student's response is true or false. If the student is to write the response in a blank space, it is better to use "+" and "0" than "+" and "-" (See Figure 6–1). Have the students draw a circle around "T" or "F" rather than write in these letters. These suggestions will make for easier and more objective scoring. If at all possible, it is best to use a separate answer sheet that can be machine-scored.

Require Application of Learning

Wherever possible, construct items so that the students are required to apply the concepts learned. This point is applicable to any type of test item, but especially to true-false items, in which the tendency is to test for acquisition of facts alone. This is one of the important factors that makes it inadvisable to use simple true-false items in measuring real achievement.

The following example, which measures memorization only, is typical of many true-false items found in teacher-made tests:

> T F x. The formula for BHP is $2 \times pi \times LNW / 33,000$.
> (Not so good)

In order to answer this item correctly, the students only have to remember a formula or definition from the textbook or as given in class by the instructor. They may know the formula without having any idea about its application in a practical situation. With a slight revision as below, this deficiency could be at least partially corrected.

> T F y. The brake horsepower of a V8 engine, which at 4600 RPM registers 135 pounds at the end of a $2\frac{1}{2}$ foot Prony brake arm, is approximately 295.
> (Better)

In this instance the students must not only know what brake horsepower is, but they must also be able to calculate it when given specifications. They would have to apply their knowledge of brake horsepower. Of course the guessing element could enter the picture, so students could get the item right without being able to apply the formula, but they would have to be pretty accurate guessers. A third alternative in this instance would be to keep the concept being tested and devise another type of item, such as completion, that would more accurately determine the level of the students' learning. It is sometimes so difficult to revise a true-false item so that it calls for application rather than memorization that other types of items should be considered.

Avoid Verbatim Statements

Another common fault when constructing true-false items is to take statements directly from books. When such a practice is carried out, it encourages students to memorize statements without understanding what they really mean or how they may be applied. Such "knowledge" is invariably temporary in nature. Statements taken out of context and placed in a test, like "sound bites" taken from a speech or interview, or short quotes from a magazine article, are often ambiguous and do not convey the true meaning intended. As a result the students are puzzled and may mark the item incorrectly even though they know or understand the concept being tested.

Use Clear Language

Use direct statements and avoid words with general meanings. Make direct comparisons. Whenever possible, use quantitative statements such as " . . . is two-thirds the . . ." rather than qualitative statements such as " . . . is better than . . ." Words with general meanings, such as "large," "great," "many," and "few," tend to make an item ambiguous to the student and should be avoided.

Poor

_____ **1.** Many computers use EISA technology.

Better

_____ **2.** The latest versions of PC-compatible computers use EISA technology.

In the first example the word *many* would probably cause a student to wonder what the item is supposed to measure. The statement is vague and indecisive. The second example is an improvement because a direct statement is used, so the meaning is much clearer. In the example following this paragraph, a single word makes the item highly ambiguous. The test maker intended that this item should be correctly marked as a true statement. The word *about* is used in a comparative sense and makes the intended meaning vague, especially to the better students. In this instance the item would be improved by dropping the word *about*.

_____ **1.** Electricity travels at about the same rate as light.

Keep Statements of Equal Length

Do not make the true statements consistently longer than the false statements. Research of a large number of teacher-made true-false tests has revealed that items containing more than 20 words were true 3 out of 4 times. In an effort to be as precise as possible, words are added and the true statements grow in length. Students soon notice this and when in doubt will mark the longer statements true.

Avoid Negative Statements

Negative statements tend to be confusing to students, and with a little effort can be revised into positive statements. As you read the example given below, note how you pause in determining whether to mark it true or false.

Poor

_____　**1.** It is not normal for students to resist learning.

Better

_____　**2.** It is normal for students to resist learning.

The first statement is false, because it *is* normal for students to resist learning. Although the answers are different for the two questions, the concept being tested is the same, and the students will answer the second one with less effort.

Be Aware of Specific Determiners

Many true-false items can be answered correctly by locating qualifying words that become specific determiners. Whenever you use such words as *no, never, always, may, should, all,* or *only,* be sure that they do not make the correct answers obvious, as in the following selected examples:

_____　**1.** A magnet is <u>always</u> used to align disks.
_____　**2.** When wordprocessing, it <u>may</u> sometimes be desirable to use the spellchecking option.
_____　**3.** Copper wire is the <u>only</u> wire used for conducting electricity.
_____　**4.** The <u>most</u> reliable car is the Reo.
_____　**5.** The angle of dwell should <u>always</u> be 16 degrees.
_____　**6.** All personal computers have at least 640k of memory.
_____　**7.** A CAT scan <u>never</u> depicts a body system as clearly as the MRI.

Teacher-made tests will provide many examples similar to the above. The important point is not to omit such words entirely, but to be careful in using them and to make sure that such words do not make the correct answer obvious. The test maker determines whether or not particular words become specific determiners.

Make the Point Obvious

There should be no question about what you are trying to measure. This does not mean that the correct answer should be obvious, but rather that the student who knows the subject matter should understand immediately what is being tested. A good practice is to have the significant part (crucial element) of the item come at the end of the statement. Sometimes this can be achieved by <u>underlining</u> the significant part of the item.

Avoid Tricky Stuff

Do not devise items that try to catch the students off guard. Such questions are poor measures of achievement. Students may know the point being measured but still not be able to detect the word or clause that really determines the correct response. Such items measure general intelligence or alertness level rather than mastery of subject matter, and their use violates fair play.

Correcting for Guessing

If you plan to correct for guessing (despite the evidence against the practice), be sure to emphasize this in the directions (See Figure 6–6). Informal teacher-made tests are not usually significantly improved by using a correction formula, but some teachers insist on doing it anyway. The chance factor involved with guessing may be too large to be disregarded, even in the informal classroom testing situation.

If a correction formula is to be used, it should be clearly indicated in the directions and the method of correction explained. Various formulas have been devised, but the one most widely used is to subtract the number wrong from the number right

PEANUTS By Schulz

PEANUTS reprinted by permission of UFS, Inc.

(right – wrong). The net result of this formula is to subtract two points for each item marked incorrectly and one point for each item omitted. It is difficult to explain to students how this practice is not a form of punishment, especially when they may have guessed correctly because they knew a little about the statement or recognized words or phrases. They could probably make the point that they should be given partial credit for knowing a little rather than being docked points for knowing a little.

Use Modified Items When Possible

This suggestion is especially applicable for comprehensive tests, such as midterm or final examinations. As explained previously, the regular true-false item can be used to advantage in certain types of instructional tests, but the inherent weakness and common abuses of the item make it a poor measure of real achievement. It may be easier to construct simple true-false items, but the other types will usually do a better job of measuring.

SUMMARY

The true-false item consists of a declaratory statement that is either true or false (right or wrong). It is widely used and often abused. There are numerous variations and modifications that help to correct certain of the inherent weaknesses.

True-false tests are easy to design, easy to score, and can be used to cover a wide range of material quickly, although the quality is often doubtful. They can be used to sample a wide range of subject matter, with students usually being able to answer three to five true-false items per minute. True-false items can be scored readily in an objective manner.

True-false items are of doubtful value for measuring achievement and they encourage guessing because of the 50–50 chance on each item. Difficulty is encountered in constructing items that are completely true or false without being obvious. Ambiguities, unimportant details, and irrelevant clues are added weaknesses of the typical true-false item. In addition, they are apt to be low in reliability, and they often measure students' reading ability rather than their knowledge of the subject matter.

DISCUSSION QUESTIONS

1. Why do you like or dislike true-false items in the tests that you are called upon to take?

2. Do you think there should be a correction for guessing when true-false items are included in a test? Why?

3. In constructing true-false items in which the student has to explain or justify the response, what difficulty is apt to be encountered?

4. Why is it a poor policy to take statements directly from books?

5. What is your description of a catch, or trick, question?

EXERCISES

1. Consider the relationship between test validity and reliability. Construct two true-false items (any type) that measure an understanding of this relationship.

2. Construct a sample true-false item that calls for reasoning on the part of the student.

3. If possible, secure a true-false test that has been prepared for a subject-matter field other than your own. See how many items you can answer because they are obvious or because there is some weakness in the construction. Such an activity will be enjoyable as well as instructive.

4. From your subject matter, construct at least twenty items such as those described in this chapter and illustrated in the figures. At least five items should be simple true-false items (Figures 6–1 to 6–8), five should be cluster true-false (Figures 6–9 and 6–10), and five should be based on a diagram (Figures 6–11 and 6–12). The final five items can be any one or several of the modified items illustrated in Figures 6–13 to 6–19. Include the directions to the students for each set of items. Prepare an answer sheet with the correct responses to each item indicated.

RESOURCES

A Reference List and Selected Bibliography

Berk, R.A., Ed. *A guide to criterion-referenced test construction.* Baltimore, MD: Johns Hopkins University Press.

Ebel, R.L. (1975, Spring) Can teachers write good true-false test items? *Journal of Educational Measurement.*

Ross, C.C. (1941). *Measurement in today's schools*, Second Edition. New York: Prentice-Hall.

▶ 7

Constructing Multiple-Choice Items

Multiple-choice items, like true-false items, can be used to test knowledge of factual information or understanding of the subject matter. They reduce the chances of guessing the correct answer from one in two (50 percent) to one in four or five (20–25 percent), and they are easy to score. Multiple-choice test items consist of a question or incomplete statement followed by several possible answers, only one of which is correct. The students must select the best or correct answer in accordance with the directions given.

In their several forms, multiple-choice items are one of the most valuable kinds of questions that can be incorporated in written tests. The remainder of this chapter is devoted to describing the uses and limitations of multiple-choice items, presenting examples of common variations, and listing points to observe in constructing multiple-choice items. In order to provide examples from as many fields as possible, the individual items contained in the examples are not necessarily from related subject-matter fields. The first item may be from one field, the second from another, and so on.

ADVANTAGES OF MULTIPLE-CHOICE ITEMS

Multiple-choice items can be designed to measure the students' ability to interpret, discriminate, select, and make application of facts or concepts learned. They can also be used to determine level of understanding, judgment, and inferential reasoning ability. For these purposes multiple-choice items are generally the most valuable of the several types of objective test items.

Multiple-choice items may be used to measure what one can *recognize*, which represents a much wider field than what one can recall or remember. Being able to recall something, however, indicates a higher order of learning than does recognition.

Multiple-choice tests can be made entirely objective and they are easily scored using a number of different types of optical scanning forms. Most students have used multiple-choice items throughout their schooling, so they are generally well acquainted with them and understand how to respond. There is not likely to be confusion unless one of the variations of the item is used without proper explanation. Further, guessing is not as much of a problem in well-constructed multiple-choice items as it is in true-false items.

Mosier, Myers, and Price (1945) suggested fourteen different types of questions that could be asked using multiple-choice items. Illustrative examples of each of those kinds of questions were provided by Micheels and Karnes (1950) and are included below because this knowledge is valuable to teachers in interpreting test results (See Chapter 12). Each of the example items measures some aspect of the concept of central tendency as used in statistics, and in each instance the correct choice is A. The A response choice is used in these examples only so that you will know the answer intended. As you will learn later in this chapter, the correct response choice should always be varied among the several choices. Notice also that each of the examples has five answer choices (A–E). Most teacher-made multiple choice items will have four choices, largely because they are that much easier and faster to construct.

1. *Questions relating to definition*, such as, "What means the same as . . . ?" or, "Which of the following statements expresses this concept in different terms?" Questions of this type assess lower-level performance, in that students are asked to recognize words or terms that they have seen or heard before.

The value determined by adding all the scores and dividing by the number of cases is known in statistics as the

A. arithmetic mean.　　　**D.** harmonic mean.
B. median.　　　　　　　**E.** average deviation.
C. mode.

2. *Questions relating to purpose*, such as, "What purpose is served by . . . ?" "What principle is exemplified by . . . ?" "This is this done because . . . ?" "What is the most important reason for . . . ?" While this type of item may also border on the recognition level, the student is required to think of reasons for some phenomenon or occurrence, rather than just recognize it.

The mean is obtained for the purpose of providing

A. a single number to represent a whole series of numbers.
B. the central point in a series.
C. a measure of group variability.
D. an indication of the most frequent response given.
E. an estimate of the relationship between two variables.

3. *Questions relating to cause*, such as, "What is the cause of . . . ?" "Under which of the following conditions is this true?" Questions of this type determine if students are able to organize or reorganize data or concepts.

From which of the following measures of central tendency will the sum of the deviations equal zero?

A. The mean
B. The mode
C. The median
D. An arbitrary origin
E. Any measure of central tendency

4. *Questions relating to effect*, such as, "What is the effect of . . . ?" "If this is done, what will happen?" "Which of the following should be done to achieve a given purpose?" Items of this type may also be used to assess the students' abilities to determine the effects of actions on their part before the action is actually taken, or, given a set of data, to predict results.

The arithmetic mean of 55 cases is 83.00. If three of the cases with values of 82, 115, and 130 are deleted from the data, the mean of the remaining 52 cases will be

A. 77.05.
B. 81.50.
C. 83.00.
D. 84.50.
E. 94.08.

5. *Questions relating to association*, such as, "What tends to occur in connection with . . . ?" Knowledge of temporal, causal, or concomitant association may be assessed with this type of item. In other words, items of this type determine how well students understand the relationship between two or more actions or phenomena.

If the distribution of scores is skewed positively, the mean will be

A. lower than the median.
B. the same as the median.
C. higher than the median.
D. relatively unaffected.
E. the same as the mode.

6. *Questions relating to recognition of error*, such as, "Which of the following constitutes an error with respect to a given situation?" This is a lower-level question because it only requires the student to recognize what is wrong or out of place in a given situation, and not explain why or how it is wrong or out of place. By analogy, this is like seeing something in which you know almost instinctively something is wrong but cannot place what the error is.

The mean should not be used as the measure of central tendency when

    A. the distribution of scores is significantly skewed.
    B. there are a large number of cases.
    C. a nontechnical report is to be prepared.
    D. the data are continuous.
    E. other statistical formulas are to be computed.

7. *Questions relating to identification of error*, such as, "What kind of error is this?" "What is the name of this error?" "What recognized principle is violated?" This kind of question, in contrast to the preceding, requires a higher level of thinking. The student is not only asked to recognize something, but is also required to recall what it is and relate it to a specific principle.

In computation of the mean of a distribution from grouped data, the sums of the deviations above and below the arbitrary origin were found to be 127 and 189, respectively. The final value for the mean was in error. Of the following possibilities, the one that is most likely to have caused the error is that the computer

    A. failed to note the correct sign in adding the mean of deviations to the assumed origin.
    B. used an assumed mean higher than the true mean.
    C. omitted some of the cases in tabulating the data.
    D. divided by the wrong number of cases.
    E. multiplied by the wrong class interval value.

8. *Questions relating to evaluation*, such as, "What is the best evaluation of . . . for a given purpose and for what reason?" As the word *evaluation* implies, this type of question involves higher-order cognitive and affective domain performance. The students not only have to perform some skill, but they are also required to place a value on the results of the performance.

When the number of cases is small, such as less than 20, and the magnitude of the values is likewise small, the use of an assumed mean in the computation of the mean can best be evaluated as

    A. less efficient than computation from actual values.
    B. likely to distort the value obtained by the introduction of a constant error.
    C. more accurate than the use of actual values.
    D. neither better nor worse than computation by other methods.
    E. applicable only if the distribution is reasonably symmetrical.

9. *Questions relating to difference*, such as, "What is the (or an) important difference between . . . ?" On the surface, this appears to be a lower-level type of question, but examination reveals that students can be required to differentiate between fairly sophisticated and complicated statements using analytic processes.

Of the following statements, the one that best characterizes the essential difference between the mean and the median as measures of the central tendency of a distribution is that the

A. magnitude of each score does not contribute proportionately to the computation of the median but does for the mean.
B. median is a point whereas the mean is a distance.
C. mean is less affected by extreme values than is the median.
D. median is easier to compute than the mean.
E. median is more generally used than the mean.

10. *Questions relating to similarity*, such as, "What is the (or an) important similarity between . . . ?" This type of question is often of the lower-level variety, but with a bit of ingenuity, students can be required to do more than just recall information.

The mean and median are both measures of

A. central tendency.
B. distance.
C. position.
D. variation.
E. relationship.

11. *Questions relating to arrangement*, such as, "In the proper order, or to achieve a given purpose or to follow a given rule, which of the following comes first or last or follows a given item?" Items such as this are often used to determine students' abilities to follow the logic of operations. They are particularly useful for any occupation where machines, instruments, or computers are used.

In the computation of the mean for data already grouped in class intervals, the most efficient first step is to

A. determine the arbitrary origin and enter the deviation values.
B. find the midpoints of the class intervals.
C. multiply the frequency in each interval by the midpoint of the interval.
D. add the column of scores.
E. find the reciprocal of the total number of cases.

12. *Questions relating to incomplete arrangement*, such as, "In the proper order, which of the following should be inserted here to complete the series?" While the example below might appear to be very complicated, it is actually assessing performance to a fairly low level of the cognitive domain (if you are a mathematics wizard!).

Items such as these may be profitably used in a variety of occupations, including all those that require following detailed procedures.

In the derivation of the formula for computing the mean from grouped data using an arbitrary origin, the following steps were taken:

A. $X' = X-A /i$
B. $\text{Sum } X = i \text{ Sum } X' + NA$
C. $\text{Sum } X / N = A + i \text{ Sum } X' / N$

The step that is implied between steps (a) and (b) is

A. solving (a) for X.
B. summing (a) over the N cases.
C. multiplying by i.
D. adding A to both terms of (a).
E. dividing by N.

13. *Questions relating to a common principle*, such as, "What is the principle?" "Which item does not belong?" "Which of the following items should be substituted?" Items of this type most often assess low- to mid-range cognitive domain performance.

All except one of the following items (arithmetic mean, median, mode, and quartile) are measures of central tendency. Of the following statistics, the one that could be substituted in the series for the item improperly included is

A. harmonic mean for quartile.
B. average deviation for mode.
C. range for quartile.
D. standard deviation for quartile.
E. 50th percentile for median.

14. *Questions relating to controversial subjects*, such as, "Although not everyone agrees on the desirability of . . . those who support its desirability do so primarily for the reason that. . . ." Items such as this require the students to analyze and synthesize knowledge, both high level performance. They also determine if students are able to take competing value statements and decide from the information given which is "best" or correct.

Although not everyone agrees that the mean is the best measure of central tendency, those who advocate its general use base their recommendation primarily on the fact that the mean

A. has the smallest sampling error.
B. is the easiest to compute.
C. is most readily understood.
D. is the most typical score.
E. is not affected by extreme scores.

It should be obvious from the preceding examples that multiple-choice items can be readily used to determine performance at the highest level of the cognitive domain. It is also possible to construct multiple-choice items that will accurately determine level of performance in the affective domain, usually to the "responding" and "valuing" levels, or the mid-range level (working knowledge) of the three-level classification system.

LIMITATIONS OF MULTIPLE-CHOICE ITEMS

The advantages of using multiple-choice items far outweigh the disadvantages, but there are some limitations in their use. For example, many test makers either do not know how or do not take the time to use these items properly. Also, they are often constructed to measure memorization only, rather than application.

It is difficult to devise items so that the distractors (the alternative or possible answers), are plausible but not correct or most desirable. The distractor statements are often obviously wrong, or in other instances they provide clues that make the correct response obvious.

When constructing multiple-choice items, it is easy to include more than one response that can be marked correctly. In other words, it is sometimes difficult to construct a good item so that one and *only* one response is the correct one. Multiple-choice tests take a lot of space—they use a good deal of paper. When spaced to provide maximum readability, it is usually only possible to get five or six items per page. In addition, multiple-choice items are time-consuming to construct.

VARIATIONS OF MULTIPLE-CHOICE ITEMS

As with the true-false item, numerous variations and modifications of multiple-choice items have been developed to capitalize on their advantages and to minimize their weaknesses. Samples of several varieties of multiple choice items are presented on the next few pages. Examples of the instructions to the students are included with each type of sample item. The examples are from different subjects, and are chronologically numbered within each item type. Keep in mind that the examples are presented as if the student is to answer directly on the test paper. The instructions will be somewhat different if a separate answer sheet is to be used.

If using the test paper as an answer sheet, it makes better sense in many ways to place answer blanks on the right of the items. Most people are right-handed, so it is easier for them to place their answers on the right after they have read the statement from left to right. This also makes it easier for a right-handed teacher to correct the items. These advantages are offset by the difficulties in placing the answer blank in an appropriate, easy-to-find place at the right of the item and for left-handed persons to answer. Again, the best solution is to use a separate answer sheet.

One Right Answer

The one right answer item is the simplest kind of multiple-choice item. The student is required to identify the *one* correct response listed among several that are totally, but not obviously, wrong. Figure 7–1 contains several examples of multiple-choice items that have only one correct answer.

Best-Answer Multiple-Choice Items

This variation of the multiple-choice item requires the student to select the correct answer or best response from a series of several responses, all of which might be plausible answers. It is perhaps the most valuable of the forms of multiple-choice items, but it has often been criticized because the selection of the best response involves judgment. But, the fact that it *does* require judgment, or inferential reasoning, or complete understanding to select the best response is the most important feature of the item. A major responsibility of good teaching in virtually every occupation is to get the students to the point where they can form judgments, draw conclusions, make close discriminations, and arrive at decisions: to be able to survive with minimal or no supervision on the job. You must teach and test for these abilities.

The best answer type of multiple-choice item may be varied to require the student to: (1) Select the two best responses from a series of possible answers, (2) indicate the worst response or the least desirable solution, or (3) indicate both the best and the worst responses. All of these variations can be employed to measure the student's ability to use logical reasoning and make application of the concepts or information learned. Figure 7–2 contains several examples of the best answer type of multiple-choice item.

Association Items

Association multiple-choice items include a word, phrase, or an illustration, followed by several choices, one of which is most closely associated with the first part. When properly constructed, association items can measure the inferential reasoning ability of the students.

All items in a block of association-type multiple-choice items should be related to the same unit of instruction if possible in order to keep the students in the same mindset. Notice how cluttered the items in Figures 7–3 and 7–4 appear. It would be much easier for the students if the answers were placed vertically under the stem word as was done in previous examples. It would make it easier when typing the item in preparing the examination.

Analogy-Type Items

The analogy item is an adaptation of a mathematical abbreviation (4:2::10:? or four is to two as ten is to ?). The student is required to discover the relationship that exists

<u>Directions:</u> Each of the questions or incomplete statements listed below is followed by several words, phrases, or series of numbers. From these, you are to choose the one that answers the question or completes the statement correctly. Place the letter of that word or phrase (A, B, C, D, or E) in the numbered blank space at the left of the item. The first item is answered as an example to follow.

   <u>D</u>   1. The primary teeth are also called the _____ teeth.

      A. adolescent

      B. incisor

      C. permanent

      D. deciduous

_____ 2. Individualized instruction should eliminate the problem of

      A. stimulating all students equally.

      B. testing each student on each lesson.

      C. having some students idle.

      D. dealing with individual differences.

_____ 3. One of the aims of individualized instruction is to provide ways for the students to

      A. be tested with the group.

      B. receive an equal amount of assistance.

      C. learn at a common rate.

      D. progress according to their own learning rate.

_____ 4. One of the purposes of the assignment sheet is to

      A. indicate experiments to be performed and understood.

      B. give information beyond that found in textbooks.

      C. help students learn how to study.

      D. teach manipulative skills beyond that learned on the job.

_____ 5. An exposure made at 1/100 second at f/8 is equivalent to

      A. 1/200 second at f/16.

      B. 1/25 second at f/16.

      C. 1/40 second at f/4.5.

      D. 1/25 second at f/4.5.

FIGURE 7–1 **One Right Answer Multiple-Choice Item**

Directions: Each of the questions or incomplete statements listed below is followed by several possible answers. Choose the answer that best answers the question or completes the statement. Place the indentifying letter of that answer (A, B, C, D, or E) in the numbered blank space at the left of the item. The first item is answered as an example.

___D___   1. A man is found unconscious in a building. There is no odor, but the building seems stuffy. The most important thing to do first is

    A. call a doctor.

    B. take him to a hospital.

    C. throw cold water on him.

    D. get him into fresh air and start CPR.

    E. rub his arms and legs.

_____   2. The Law of Effect is an expression of the relationship between success and pleasant feelings. Which of the following is an application of this principle in the teaching of a skill-oriented class?

    A. The first assignments for a new class should be relatively simple.

    B. The first efforts of the student should result in a completed project with little attention paid to the proper skills.

    C. The teacher should do most of the operations for the beginning student in order that the first project may be successful.

    D. Students will do little work if they do not experience pleasant feelings.

    E. Students will not learn if they experience unpleasant feelings in the first activities of the class.

_____   3. The most important difference between standardized achievement tests and informal, teacher-made tests is that the standardized tests

    A. have been constructed by experts in test construction and subject matter.

    B. have a far more adequate sampling of the subject matter of the course.

    C. have been proven through item analysis.

    D. furnish norms that fit the classroom situation.

    E. are generally more valid in the classroom situation.

FIGURE 7–2   **Best-Answer Multiple-Choice Items**

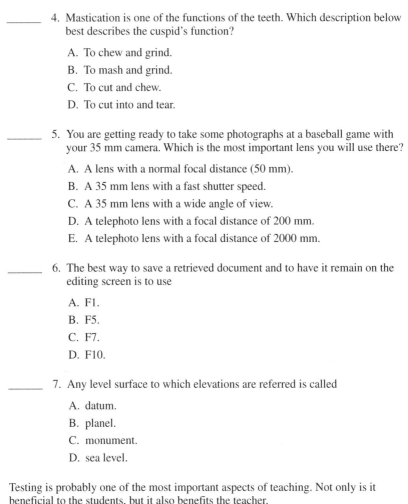

_____ 4. Mastication is one of the functions of the teeth. Which description below best describes the cuspid's function?

    A. To chew and grind.

    B. To mash and grind.

    C. To cut and chew.

    D. To cut into and tear.

_____ 5. You are getting ready to take some photographs at a baseball game with your 35 mm camera. Which is the most important lens you will use there?

    A. A lens with a normal focal distance (50 mm).

    B. A 35 mm lens with a fast shutter speed.

    C. A 35 mm lens with a wide angle of view.

    D. A telephoto lens with a focal distance of 200 mm.

    E. A telephoto lens with a focal distance of 2000 mm.

_____ 6. The best way to save a retrieved document and to have it remain on the editing screen is to use

    A. F1.

    B. F5.

    C. F7.

    D. F10.

_____ 7. Any level surface to which elevations are referred is called

    A. datum.

    B. planel.

    C. monument.

    D. sea level.

Testing is probably one of the most important aspects of teaching. Not only is it beneficial to the students, but it also benefits the teacher.

Before teachers can even think about testing, they must have a properly constructed syllabus. Each weekly assignment must be clearly and concisely defined. Students must have no doubts as to what the objectives are and the conditions and criteria applicable to each. Once these are defined, instruction can begin that has the sole purpose of accomplishing an observable behavior change.

The design of the test must complement the learning objectives. It must encompass the specific subject matter, yet it must be discriminating enough to show differences in the amount learned by the students. This is a helpful aid for future instruction. In classes such as wordprocessing, the psychomotor performances can be

FIGURE 7–2 (CONTINUED)   **Best-Answer Multiple-Choice Items** objectively scored by evaluating completed documents for errors and time. The cognitive knowledge to manipulate the software can also be measured through written examinations.

_____ 8. You have typed the document above and realized that the second paragraph should be in bold for emphasis. Which of the following commands would be easiest to use to accomplish that task?

   A. Block the area and press F6.
   B. Place the cursor on the first letter of the paragraph and press F6.
   C. Place the cursor on the first letter of the paragraph and press F8.
   D. Block the area and press F8.

NOTE: A number of items could be made from the illustration above. For example, words could be intentionally misspelled and the students asked the commands to find and correct them. The possibilities are only limited by the imagination of the instructor.

FIGURE 7–2 (CONTINUED)   **Best-Answer Multiple-Choice Items**

between the first two parts of the item and then apply this relationship to the third and fourth parts. The third part is given, but the fourth must be selected from the several choices on the basis of the relationship existing between the first two parts. This type of item has been used more often in intelligence testing than in classroom or teacher-made achievement tests, but it does measure to high levels of the cognitive domain.

Reverse Multiple-Choice

The reverse multiple-choice item differs from other forms in that the students are required to choose the *poorest or wrong response* from among several correct responses. This variation is especially suitable for material in which there are several correct or best responses. It has two features: (1) It is usually easier to construct three or four responses that are true about a general fact than to make several that are plausible but still wrong, and (2) in deciding on their response, students seem to consider more of the choices listed after such items. If this is true, then such items might be said to demand more interpretation and discrimination on the part of the student, both high level cognitive domain behaviors.

It is not a good idea to place a section of reverse multiple-choice items immediately after regular multiple-choice items in a test because the students are apt to be

Directions: The first word in the following groups of items is closely related to another word in the same item. Select the word to which the first word is most closely related. Place the identifying letter of the word in the blank space at the left. The first item is answered as an example.

  B   x. Surface: (A) view, (B) mesial, (C) cheek, (D) dentin

        1. Back saw: (A) rough, (B) framing, (C) finish, (D) forming

        2. Amenity: (A) towels, (B) blankets, (C) soap, (D) shampoo

        3. Market segment: (A) resort, (B) convention, (C) boatel, (D) luxury

        4. Electrical fire: (A) Class A, (B) Class B, (C) Class C, (D) Class D

        5. Peripheral: (A) night, (B) side, (C) color, (D) depth

        6. Hyoid: (A) larynx, (B) sternum, (C) ear, (D) foot, (E) wrist

        7. Enamel: (A) dentin, (B) pulp, (C) outer surface, (D) inner surface

FIGURE 7–3   **Association Multiple-Choice Items**

Directions: In the following items, determine the relationship between the first two parts of the item. Then apply this relationship to the third and fourth parts by selecting the proper choice (A, B, C, D, or E) to go with the third part. Place the letter of your choice in the blank space at the left. The first two items are answered as examples:

  D   x. 4:2::10:?: (A) 20, (B) 16, (C) 8, (D) 5, (E) 3

  C   x. Hammer: peen :: blade: ?
           (A) claw, (B) jaw, (C) tooth, (D) set, (E) pincer

        1. Mesial: distal :: labial: ?
           (A) buccal, (B) lingual, (C) occlusal, (D) distal

        2. Sampling is to comprehensiveness as item analysis is to:
           (A) reliability, (B) ease of administration, (C) subjectivity,
           (D) discrimination, (E) objectivity

        3. Printing: Gutenberg :: Personal Computing: ?
           (A) Dvorak, (B) Osborne, (C) Wang, (D) Peoples, (E) Cobol

        4. Digoxin: Cardiotonic :: Lidocaine: ?
           (A) anticonvulsant, (B) calcium channel blocker,
           (C) coronary vasodilator, (D) antiarrhythmic

FIGURE 7–4   **Analogy Multiple-Choice Items**

confused when, after selecting the best response in one set of items, they are confronted immediately with a similar set of items requiring the opposite type of response. There is some evidence that reverse multiple-choice items confuse learners, especially when regular items are a standard feature of the tests given in any one course. These items should be used with caution and thoroughly analyzed and evaluated after each test administration. See Figure 7–5 for examples of reverse multiple-choice items.

Directions: Each of the questions or incomplete statements listed below is followed by several answers. All but one of the answers are correct. One is wrong. You are to pick out the one that is wrong or false. Place the letter of that choice (A, B, C, D, or E) in the numbered blank space at the left of the item. The first item is answered as an example.

   D   x. The cementum is a bonelike substance

        A. that enables attachment of teeth to the jaw.

        B. that is the softest of the hard structures of teeth.

        C. that covers the roots of the teeth.

        D. that lies next to and protects the pulp chamber.

        1. The major reasons for professional licensure are to

        A. insure uniformity of preparation.

        B. prevent known criminals from practicing.

        C. keep undesirables out.

        D. provide public assurances of quality.

        2. In an electric circuit with capacitance

        A. there is an opposition to any change in voltage.

        B. the current phase is affected by voltage lagging current.

        C. the current flowing varies with the frequency of the supply voltage.

        D. after initial charging, direct current will flow in the circuit.

        E. after initial charging, alternating current will flow in the circuit.

        3. Some of the more common ROM BIOS programs used include

        A. AMI.

        B. Award.

        C. Phoenix.

        D. Intel.

FIGURE 7–5   **Reverse Multiple-Choice Items**

CONSTRUCTING MULTIPLE-CHOICE ITEMS

The following pages contain some general rules to follow in constructing multiple-choice items. Many of the rules are also applicable to other types of items.

The Stem Should Contain a Central Problem

"Stem" in this instance refers to the first part of the item, or the introductory statement or question. It is sometimes called the "problem" or the "lead." The remainder of the item may be referred to as "choices," "alternatives," "answers," "options," "distractors," or "possible responses." The stem should not be merely an incomplete statement followed by four or five true-false statements, only one of which is true.

The distractors should be plausible answers to a single problem or introductory question. They should call for discrimination on the part of the student in order to obtain the best measure of the student's real understanding of the point in question. A central problem is necessary in a well-constructed multiple-choice item, but it is only the first part of the item. Having a central problem does not of itself guarantee that the item will measure application of the material being tested.

The central problem may be in the form of a direct question, or it may be an incomplete statement. The direct question form will usually require more words, although it is likely to be less ambiguous. In using a direct question the choices tend to be more homogeneous, and irrelevant clues are less likely to occur in the problem. Most items will lend themselves to either approach. For beginning test makers, it is suggested that the central problem first be stated in the form of a direct question. It may later be changed to an incomplete statement, but in most instances the direct question will suffice.

The Item Should Be Practical and Realistic

The test item should not be academic and artificial (as so many items are). It should demand knowledge and understanding that the student must have or use as a part of everyday living or on the job. It should not be designed to measure innate intelligence (unless you are developing an intelligence test).

Poor (too academic)

_____ Which of the following is the formula to use in determining needed horsepower?

A. $L \times W / 33,000 \times T$
B. $L \times W \times T / 31,000$
C. $31,000 \times L / W \times T$
D. $L \times F / 33,000 \times T$

Better (practical)

_____ How much horsepower is needed to pull a stalled 2,000-pound automobile 5,000 feet in 6 minutes?

A. 5.05
B. 50.05
C. 100.5
D. 505.0

In the item asking for the correct formula the student is very apt to say, "So what?" and would be justified in doing so. It is doubtful that anyone would ever need the ability to recite such a formula, but that is all the item would measure. It is unrealistic and artificial, because anyone needing such a formula and having the skills to calculate it would surely have a reference book handy. If the course objective called for the students' ability to use the formula, it would be accomplished much better with a practical problem, as in the second example.

Poor

_____ An oblique drawing may be defined as being

A. the same as an isometric drawing.
B. similar to an isometric drawing.
C. closely related to a perspective drawing.
D. similar to a cabinet drawing.
E. similar to an orthographic projection.

  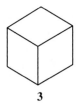

1   2   3   4   5

Better

_____ Which of the above drawings of a cube is known as an *oblique* drawing?

A. 1
B. 2
C. 3
D. 4
E. 5

The first example concerning an oblique drawing is also academic and might measure reading ability better than it does knowledge of drawing types. If it is necessary for the students to be able to identify an oblique drawing, it would be much more practical to use illustrations, as in the second example. If it is essential for the students to know and understand an oblique drawing, a still better measure would be to have them actually construct a drawing.

Items that are trivial or almost useless when viewed in the light of practicality are also closely allied to academic and unrealistic items. As an example of this point, consider two examples from the occupation of interior design:

Poor (no central problem)

_____ The primary colors are

    A. red, green, yellow.
    B. orange, blue, green.
    C. yellow, blue, green.
    D. red, yellow, blue.
    E. red, blue, orange.

Better

_____ You are on an assignment and the client wants you to match some green paint. It is necessary to mix the paint. Which of the following statements best expresses the procedure to follow in creating the mix?

    A. Apply blue paint first, then yellow.
    B. Apply red paint, then yellow.
    C. Apply yellow paint, then blue.
    D. Apply yellow paint, then red.
    E. Apply red paint, then blue.

A student could memorize the primary colors and answer the first item correctly without having a practical understanding of what to do with the information. In the second example it is necessary for the student to apply an understanding of primary and secondary colors in solving a practical problem. It also measures an understanding of the procedure followed in actually mixing the paints. An item measuring more than one point of knowledge is not undesirable in an achievement test, but in a test of subject mastery, each item should measure one specific point.

The Stated Problem Should Be Specific, Clear, and as Brief as Possible

There should be no question in the student's mind as to what the problem is. It should be as simple as possible and be readily understandable. The item should not contain information that is not relevant.

Poor

_____ Control is defined as that degree of influence that an officer of the law must exert over a resisting violator in order to

A. take him or her to prison.
B. take him or her to court for arraignment.
C. take him or her safely into custody.
D. take him or her back to his or her home.

Better

_____ Control is defined as that degree of influence that an officer must exert over violators in order to take them

A. to prison.
B. to court.
C. safely into custody.
D. home.

The first example above can be criticized in several ways: (1) It is not as simple as it might be; (2) the preliminary statement contains irrelevant information that does not add to the effectiveness of the problem; (3) there is needless repetition in each of the choices; and (4) an unnecessary amount of time would be consumed in answering the item. In this particular instance the objective could be measured more effectively and in a shorter time by revising the item to read as in the second example.

It will not always be possible or desirable to make each item as brief as the second example above. The items must be considered in terms of all the suggestions presented here. Brevity and simplicity are two of these suggestions, but in making the items brief and simple, the other features should not be excluded. In some instances there will be information in the central problem that appears irrelevant to the casual reader, but in reality may be very important in the selection of the right choice.

Illustrations Are Often Useful in Presenting the Central Problem

This statement is especially true in devising items concerning technical processes, tools, machines, understanding of drawings, and similar problems. A good general rule is to use an illustration whenever possible. In most cases this will help to make the item more practical and realistic and therefore more effective. Office copy machines and computer programs greatly simplify the process of using illustrations in tests.

In the first example below the central problem would be confusing, to say the least. Most students would have to stop and consider the several word meanings in an effort to obtain a mental picture of the piece of siding in question. The example would take unnecessary time. The student might mark the wrong response while knowing the point being tested. This example would tend to measure intelligence as well as achievement. All these criticisms disappear in the case of the second example.

Poor

_____ Horizontal siding made with a slanting cut that intersects two perpendicular surfaces but not two parallel surfaces is properly called

  A. anzac.
  B. bevel.
  C. dolly varden.
  D. drop.

Better

_____ In the drawing below, the siding marked "1" is properly called

  A. anzac.
  B. bevel.
  C. dolly varden.
  D. drop.

Sometimes a single illustration will provide material for several items, as was shown in item number 8 of Figure 7–2 earlier in this chapter.

These two examples could be augmented by many other sample items that show the advantage of using illustrations in describing the central problem. In selecting or preparing illustrations for your multiple-choice items, two important points should be kept in mind: Keep the illustrations as simple as possible, and make them clear. Notice that the response pattern in the two items above could be altered to use less space by placing the responses in two columns. This is appropriate when the answers are as short as these are.

Have at Least Four and Preferably Five Possible Answers (Choices)

When there are fewer than four choices, the item is not much better than a true-false question because it is easier to guess the correct response. In answering the item below, any intelligent student would discard choice C immediately. That would leave only two choices, with a 50–50 chance of guessing the correct response. If it is possible to prepare only two or three good choices, use another type of item to do the measuring.

_____ When fastening boards with nails, the nails should be driven

    A. in line with the grain.
    B. staggered.
    C. the handiest way.

In certain instances it may be desirable to include six or seven choices, but these occasions will be rare.

Make All Responses Plausible

If a response is obviously wrong, it might as well be left out, for an intelligent student can answer such an item by a process of elimination. All the possible answers (or distractors) should be worded in such a manner that the student must know the subject manner in order to select the correct response. The distractors should be plausible—they should lead the uninformed away from the correct answer.

Using obviously wrong responses is a common fault exhibited by beginning test makers. The example in the previous section includes one response (C) that is illustrative of this point. Because of the obviously wrong answer the guessing factor becomes very prominent. Consider the following item taken from a teacher-made test. Whether or not you are acquainted with the field being tested, you will probably be able to choose the correct response, choice (C), by a simple process of elimination.

_____ If you think your boss has harassed you, you should first tell your

    A. mother.
    B. father.
    C. supervisor's supervisor.
    D. clergy person.

In the next example, from a course for receptionists, at least two of the choices (C and D) could be eliminated immediately because of their obviously wrong nature. It is quite likely also that the correct answer could be determined through logical reasoning by an intelligent person who knows nothing at all about being a receptionist or what receptionists do. The point to be emphasized here is to check each item to make sure that none of the choices is obviously wrong.

_____ People who call during business hours have a right to expect

    A. instant action.   **C.** delays.
    B. courtesy and efficiency.   **D.** anger and curtness.

Avoid Irrelevant Clues

One common fault in this respect is to have the correct response consistently longer or consistently shorter than the distractors. The correct response must often be an expanded statement in order to make it correct. The better students become aware of such defects and mark the correct answer by looking at the structure of the choices rather than the meaning. In the first example below, the students may or may not be aware of the teacher's habits regarding length of choices. However, they may remember vaguely something said in class about an "error," and because of the long explanation required in choice C, they would tend to choose that response without knowing what the error really referred to.

_____   The electrons in a current flow

    A. from positive to negative.
    B. from negative to positive.
    C. actually from negative to positive, but due to an early error, we say they flow from positive to negative.
    D. whichever way the circuit is connected.
    E. along lines of least resistance.

In the example below, from the field of auto mechanics, the correct answer is, again, significantly longer than the rest. In this instance the choices could be lengthened without much difficulty, but the best procedure would be to revise the entire item by providing a central problem that is more realistic and practical.

_____   One of the most common causes of piston trouble is

    A. warped piston.
    B. piston slap.
    C. deposit of carbon on the piston.
    D. scored pistons.

In making multiple-choice items, then, be sure to keep the several choices about the same length. At the same time, check the grammatical construction of each item. Faulty grammar is another common weakness. Certain choices may be *automatically* discarded because of the grammar, as in the following example:

_____   A boring tool has a tendency to spring

    A. up.
    B. down.
    C. toward the top.
    D. not to spring at all.

In this item choices A and C mean the same thing. This reduces the possible answers to three. Many students would note the grammatical inconsistency of choice D, simply because it does not "read right" with the incomplete statement. This would narrow the choices to two, "up" or "down," and the item would be no more reliable than a true-false question.

In the following example you will be able to detect at least two of the wrong *distractors* merely by reading the introductory statement before each of the choices:

_____   Greater sensitivity can be obtained

    A. by a detector tube followed by two stages of audio-free amplification.
    B. by a detector tube preceded by two stages of R.F. amplification.
    C. by T.R.F.
    D. superheterodyne.
    E. class-A type.

Probably the maker of the above item worked diligently on the first choice, which was to serve as a decoy. Then the correct response was added. After that things must have begun to get difficult, it was getting real late in the evening, or nature was calling, for the last two choices do not even begin to be grammatically consistent.

These examples indicate what is meant by irrelevant clues. There are many variations of this weakness, and the better students detect such clues almost immediately. Such faults can be corrected if you are careful in checking each item.

Place the Choices at the End of the Incomplete Statement

This practice (instead of leaving a blank space in the middle of the stem) makes for continuity of reading and is less confusing for the student. When blanks are left near the beginning or the middle of the statement students must read part way, then skip over the choices to see what they are supposed to do, and finally come back to the several choices to determine the correct answer. With very little effort, items written in this fashion can be revised to include the choices at the end.

List Each Choice on a Separate Line

This takes more paper, but it is much easier for students to read and follow. For informal classroom tests it is best to identify each response with an upper-case letter (A, B, C, D, E). When figures (1, 2, 3, 4, 5) or lowercase letters (a, b, c, d, e) are used, it is sometimes difficult to determine just what the student has placed in the blank space, because several of the characters are similar in appearance and the student who is vague about the correct response may deliberately write a *5* that looks something like a *3* or a *c* that somewhat resembles an *e*. It is much better for student response clarity to use a separate answer sheet. Most answer sheets designed for machine scoring require the students to fill in a bubble, eliminating this problem altogether. If you make your own answer sheet, it is a simple matter to list the item numbers, followed by A B C D E. In this way, it is possible to create several versions of answer sheets, one for ten-item tests, one for fifteen items, one for twenty-five, and so on.

Put Series of Elements in Order

If the choices contain figures, dates, or numbers, such elements may be in ascending or descending order but they should be in *some* order. This makes it easier for the students to select their response. Use Arabic numerals as shown in the example, rather than spelling out the numbers as "one," "two," and so on.

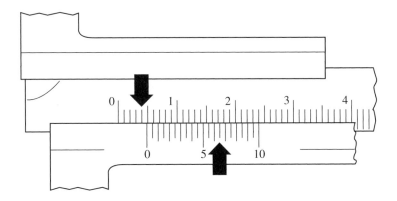

_____ What is the correct reading on the vernier caliper shown above?

A. .046	**A.** 5.03
B. 4.07	**B.** 4.65
C. 4.65	**C.** .046
D. 5.03	**D.** 5.16
E. 5.16	**E.** 4.07
(this)	*(not this)*

Scatter the Correct Responses

Make sure that the correct responses do not follow any particular pattern. It is easy to comply with this suggestion when the items are checked prior to duplication. Most computer test making programs will randomly distribute the correct responses, but this is not always a feature.

Be Sure to Make Clear When a Negative Response Is Desired

Perhaps the easiest way to emphasize the negative choice is to capitalize or underline the words that characterize the item (<u>poorest</u>, <u>not</u>, <u>no</u>, <u>least</u>, and so on). The following examples illustrate this procedure:

_____   If you were teaching a class the correct marks to use in . . . , which one of the following would <u>not</u> be included?

_____   Which one of the following <u>IS NOT</u> an example of a . . . ?

Do Not Use a Multiple-Choice Item if a Simpler Type Will Work

This suggestion is made with respect to that type of information where there is only one correct response that can be written down with one word or figure. As an illustration of this point, the multiple-choice sample test item regarding telephone callers used in a previous example might be rewritten as a simple recall (completion) item and be much more effective, as the item below shows.

_____   People who call during business hours have a right to expect _____?

SUMMARY

Multiple-choice items consist of a question or incomplete statement followed by several possible answers, from which the test taker selects the correct one. The item may take several forms. Students may be required to select the one correct answer; they may be asked to choose the best answer, the worst, or both. The item may be constructed in the form of an analogy, or it may call for association. When well constructed, the multiple-choice item is one of the best, if not *the* best, of the objective test items. Some suggestions follow for use in constructing multiple-choice items:

1. The stem of the item should contain a central problem.
2. The item should be practical and realistic.
3. The stated problem should be specific, clear, and as brief as possible.
4. Illustrations are sometimes useful in presenting the central problem.
5. Have at least four and preferably five answers (choices).
6. Include no responses that are obviously wrong.
7. Avoid the inclusion of irrelevant clues.
8. Place the choices at the end of the incomplete statement.
9. List each choice on a separate line.
10. When the choices include a series of figures, put these in order.
11. Scatter the correct responses.

12. When a negative response is desired, be sure to make this clear.

13. Do not use a multiple-choice item if a simpler type will be sufficient.

DISCUSSION QUESTIONS

1. What are some other names that might be more descriptive of the multiple-choice type of item?

2. What do you think about the best-answer type of item that calls for discrimination on the part of the student? In other words, what has been your reaction when you have taken this type of test? Should this have any bearing on the type of items you put in your tests? Why or why not?

3. Why is it a good idea to think in terms of a central problem when starting out to construct a multiple-choice item?

4. What do you think about including a section of reverse multiple-choice items in your tests?

5. How can regular multiple-choice items be constructed to measure in the same manner as reverse multiple-choice items?

6. What are the faults to be avoided in constructing multiple-choice items?

EXERCISES

1. Construct twenty multiple-choice items, following closely the suggestions contained in this chapter. Use illustrations such as those shown in the text discussion of the rules for constructing multiple choice items for at least two of your items. Start out by first examining the specific objective you wish to measure, then create items to measure the completion of that objective. (You do not have to include the objectives when you turn the items in to the instructor.) Include instructions to the student for each kind of item that you create. Direct the students to use a separate answer sheet, and design and include the answer sheet with all answers indicated.

While you are completing this assignment, make plans to start a file of good test items.

RESOURCES

A Reference List and Selected Bibliography

Gronlund, N.E. (1973). *Preparing criterion-referenced tests for classroom instruction.* New York: Macmillan.

Haladyna, T.M., & Downing, S.M. (1989). A taxonomy of multiple-choice item-writing rules. *Applied Measurement in Education, 2* (1), 37–50.

Micheels, W.J., & Karnes, M.R. (1950). *Measuring educational achievement.* New York: McGraw-Hill.

Mosier, C.I., Myers, M.C., & Price, H.G. (1945, Autumn). Suggestions for the construction of multiple-choice test items. *Educational and Psychological Measurement, 5,* 261–271.

Roid, G.H., & Haladyna, T.M. (1980). The emergence of an item-writing technology. *Review of Educational Research, 50,* 293–314.

▶ 8

Constructing Completion Items

Completion test items consist of a statement with one or more key words missing and blanks left in their place. Students are required to "fill in the blanks" to complete the statement correctly. If the question is one that can be answered very briefly, it may be put in the form of a completed question, followed by a blank space.

Completion items test the students' ability to recall information, rather than to recognize it in context. They are good to use when students must be able to remember facts, words, or symbols. It is very difficult to guess the correct answer with completion items. It is, however, difficult to create statements that call for only one correct answer. There are only slight differences between certain of the item types illustrated in this chapter. It is sufficient to remember that nearly all are classified as *recall-type* items.

ADVANTAGES OF COMPLETION ITEMS

Completion, or recall, items can be used to measure the retention of specific points. They demand accurate information from the students, are relatively easy to construct, and are applicable to virtually any field in which students are required to remember information.

The common types of completion items are used primarily in measuring who, what, when, and where types of information. They can be substituted for recognition items when it is desired to have the students recall outright the information being tested. For example, the identification type of item explained later in the chapter can often be used in place of matching exercises, with only minor revisions.

The variations of completion items can be used effectively to sample a wide range of subject matter, including the application of certain knowledge, as in detecting the errors in a drawing. The problem and situation type of item is especially valuable for measuring certain types of subject matter involving arithmetic computations, use of formulas, use of measuring instruments, and similar abilities. Completion items tend to have a high discriminating value, that is, they separate those who have mastered the material from those who have not. Because they discriminate so well, the guessing factor is minimized as well because the students either know the answers or they don't.

LIMITATIONS OF COMPLETION ITEMS

Because simple types of completion items are easy to construct, there is a tendency for them to be used excessively, resulting in an overemphasis on verbal facility and the memorization of facts. Because of the nature and construction of many items, they often provide a better measure of native intelligence than of mastery of the subject matter in a given course.

Unless care is exercised in constructing completion items, the scoring very easily becomes subjective. It is also difficult to measure complete understanding of a subject with the simple types of completion items. Completion items may be time-consuming for the students to write the answers. Also, they may know the material being tested but have difficulty in recalling the exact word needed to fill in a certain blank.

SIMPLE COMPLETION ITEMS

Simple completion items such as those shown in Figures 8–1 through 8–3 require the students to supply a word, figure, or date from memory. The word(s) may come at the end of a statement, they may be an answer to a direct question, or they may be associated with another word or phrase. The example immediately below illustrates these three approaches, using the same subject matter.

_____ 1. Any level surface to which elevations are referred is called _____.
_____ 1. What is the surface to which elevations are referred called?
_____ 1. Elevations

Sentence-completion items usually require the students to recall and supply one or more key words that have been omitted from statements. The words, when inserted in the appropriate blanks, make the statements complete, meaningful, and true. The statements may be isolated and unrelated, or they may be combined to form short paragraphs that carry a continuous line of thought. The items in Figure 8–4 are obviously from different subject areas.

The items in Figure 8–5 are also considered sentence completion items, but they

Directions: Each of the people listed below has made an important contribution to the field of computing. Identify each of them by writing a <u>few</u> descriptive words regarding their contribution in the blank space provided.

1. Wozniak _____
2. Osborne _____
3. Wang _____
4. Norton _____
5. Amdahl _____

FIGURE 8–1   **Several-Word Answer**

Directions: Each of the statements below contains a blank space at or near the end of the statement. You are to supply the missing word. Write your word in the blank space at the left of the item.

_____   1. The task of starting a computer is known as the _____ process.

_____   2. The primary output device of a personal computer is known as the _____.

_____   3. The system hardware device used for inputting data is called _____.

FIGURE 8–2   **Blank Space at the End**

Directions: Answer each of the following questions by writing the correct answer in the blank space at the left.

_____   1. Who invented the DRAM chip?
_____   2. What is the basic unit of memory called?
_____   3. What is the unit of capacitance?
_____   4. What formula is used to find the circumference of a circle?
_____   5. What instrument is used to measure the angle of supination?

FIGURE 8–3   **Answer a Question**

Directions: Each of the blank spaces in the following statements indicates the place of an omitted word. Complete the meaning of each statement by writing the correct word in the corresponding numbered blank at the left.

_____ 1. The leading competitor of the United States in the electronics market is _____.

_____ 2. The published room rate is called the _____ rate.

_____ 3. The effect on operation if FL4 did not energize would be no _____.

_____ 4. A thermometer should be rinsed in _____ water.

_____ 5. Before use, a thermometer should be shaken down to below _____ degrees Fahrenheit.

_____ 6. There are two types of taping, typical and _____.

_____ 7. Forest land and resource management is called _____.

_____ 8. The leading agricultural crop in California is _____.

_____ 9. The green coloring substance of plants is called _____.

_____ 10. The NPK of sulfate of ammonia is _____.

_____ 11. To enhance the prompt size, type prompt- _____.

_____ 12. A person in shock will have cold and _____ skin.

_____ 13. The term commonly used that means death beginning in the brain is _____.

FIGURE 8-4   **Sentence-Completion Items**

Directions: Complete the following exercise by filling in the proper word (or words) in the several blank spaces.

Identification and proper use of hand tools is an essential skill of automotive mechanics. Wrenches with one box and one open end are called _____ wrenches. Tools that are designed to fit all the way around a bolt or nut are called _____ wrenches, while those with an opening at one end are termed _____. Screwdrivers are of two basic types: _____ and _____. When wrenches or screwdrivers will not fit, _____ should be used.

FIGURE 8-5   **Blank Spaces in a Paragraph**

are all run together in a paragraph. Another variation of the example shown in Figure 8–5—which would be much easier for students to take and the teacher to score—is to number the blank spaces and require the students to write their answers in blank spaces at the left, as shown in Figure 8–4, or on a separate answer sheet.

PROBLEM OR SITUATION ITEMS

Ordinary arithmetic problems are examples of simple recall-type items. Variations can be devised requiring the students to do such things as complete a formula, fill in missing parts, or use a formula in solving a specified problem. The situation item shown in Figures 8–6 and 8–7 may require the students to indicate their response by making a simple sketch or by a response in narrative form. Situation items and the items shown in Figures 8–8 and 8–9 are very similar to the simple recall or sentence-completion type.

IDENTIFICATION ITEMS

Another type of recall item that might be classified with completion items is the identification item, which may be used to measure the students' ability to indicate the proper names of such things as tools, mechanical units, symbols, instruments, or specific parts. These items may also be used to measure the ability of the students to analyze special difficulties or identify errors in a drawing or picture. (Pictures or drawings are almost essential in written identification tests—see Figure 8–10—so reproduction is sometimes a problem.) Identification test items measure recognition and recall. Sometimes teachers require students to state briefly the purpose or use of each identified item in addition to naming it. This practice determines the depth of

---

Directions: Analyze the situation presented in each of the items listed below. Write each answer in the blank space at the left.

_____ 1. The rectal temperature of a patient is 101.2 degrees. What will the oral temperature read?

_____ 2. The respiration rate to pulse rate ratio is 1 to 4. The patient's pulse rate is 100 beats per minute. What is the respiration rate?

_____ 3. The turf grass appears to be light green in color. What does it lack?

_____ 4. An area in your landscaping requires a hardy, fast-growing shade tree. What would be a good selection?

FIGURE 8–6   **Situation Completion Items**

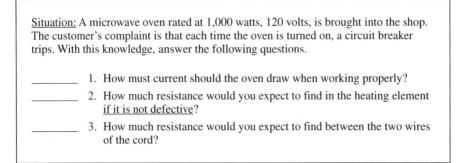

FIGURE 8–7   **Multiple Questions, One Situation**

understanding, but students who have difficulty expressing themselves verbally sometimes falter on these items.

Another type of test, called an *object test*, is similar to the identification test but uses actual objects, such as tools, instruments, and materials. These test items require the student to recognize something and then supply a name or function. In one variation the teacher holds actual objects, such as tools or parts, and the students write the names or functions on an answer sheet. In another variation, the objects to be identified are placed at numbered stations in the classroom and the students are directed from one station to another where they write the names or functions of the material displayed. Object tests may be used primarily as instructional devices, or they may be used as sections of comprehensive examinations.

Object tests may be used to determine if students have the ability to identify kinds, grades, and sizes of materials, instruments, and tools and to differentiate their uses. The object test can also be used to determine knowledge of correct adjustment of tools and instruments. Some manipulative performance may be involved in object tests, but the focus is usually limited to the measurement of understanding. Object tests are developed much like the completion items discussed in this chapter, but

> Directions: Complete the following formulas by writing in the missing words, figures, terms, or symbols. Place your answers in the blank space at the left.
>
> _____   1. Circumference of a circle = ?
> _____   2. Arithmetic Mean = ?
> _____   3. RPM = CX × _____?

FIGURE 8–8   **Complete Formulas**

Directions: The drawing below contains 15 numbered items. Place the name of the structural member indicated by each numbered line in the corresponding space on your answer sheet.

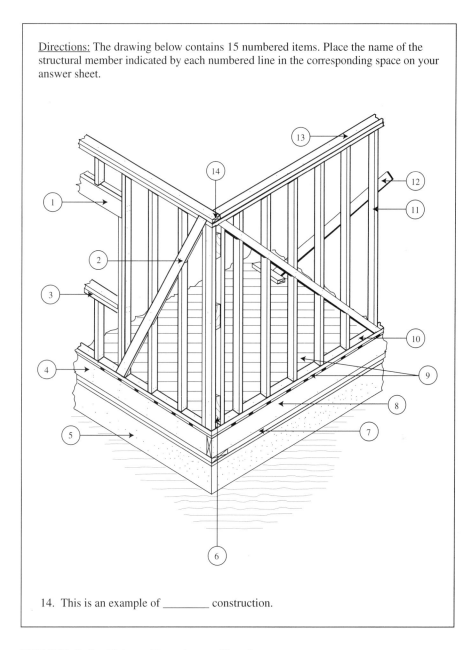

14. This is an example of _____ construction.

FIGURE 8–9 **Using a Drawing or Sketch**

Directions: Listed below are several abbreviations or common symbols used in statistics. You are to write the proper meaning in the blank space at the left.

_____ 1. M or $\overline{X}$

_____ 2. Σ (Sigma)

_____ 3. Q

_____ 4. S.D.

_____ 5. !

Directions: Shown below are various abbreviations, or symbols, used in the Periodic Table of elements. Write the proper name for each element in the blank space at the left of the symbol.

_____ 1. Fe

_____ 2. Au

_____ 3. Sb

_____ 4. Na

_____ 5. Rn

Directions: Identify the parts of the drum brake assembly shown. Write your answers in the corresponding numbered blank space on your answer sheet.

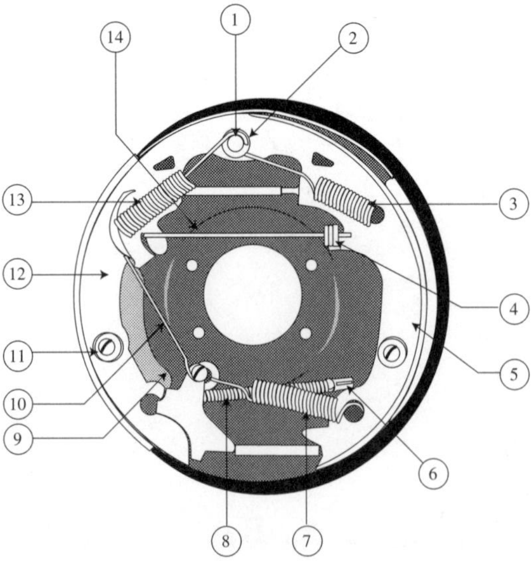

FIGURE 8–10 **Identification Items (Three Variations)**

they are administered following the same procedures described in Chapter 11 for performance tests.

CONTROLLED COMPLETION ITEMS

The controlled completion item is a variation that requires the students to recognize and select from a list of possible responses the correct answer for each blank provided. These items are more recognition items than recall, and are similar to multiple-choice and matching items. The longer the list that is used, such as in Figure 8–11, the closer these items become to matching items. Controlled completion can be used effectively to measure the students' ability to make close discriminations, and they are well suited to measurement along a continuous line of thought. Scoring is totally objective.

On the surface, controlled completion items appear to be relatively easy to construct. In reality, it is very difficult to construct these items so that they are valid and

---

Directions: Several incomplete statements are listed below. Each blank space indicates that a word or group of words has been left out. From the list given below the statements, select the word or group of words that will make each statement correct and write these words in the appropriate space on your answer sheet. Use each word or group only once.

1. The hydraulic components of a disk brake system are housed in the _____.
2. To delay pressure build-up to the front brakes, a _____ valve is used.
3. Brakes that use a wedging action of the shoes to help apply the brakes are called _____ brakes.
4. To maintain the correct proportion of pressure between the front disk and rear drum brakes, a _____ valve is used.
5. The part of the disk brake system that turns or rotates with the wheels is called the _____.

antiskid system	caliper
coefficient of friction	constant-velocity
disk brakes	oscillation
metering	Pascal's Law
ball bearings	proportioning
rotor	self-adjusters
self-energized	

FIGURE 8–11   **Controlled Completion Items**

reliable. Too often, controlled completion items can be answered by the student who knows nothing more than the simple rules pertaining to grammatical construction and English usage.

It can be seen from this example that controlled completion items are very similar to matching items as described in the next chapter. The list of words or phrases from which choices are to be made should include several extra words or phrases. There should be at least three plausible responses for each blank, but only one that is correct. Notice in Figure 8–11 that the blank spaces in the items are too small for the students to write their answers in. It is not necessary to leave several small blanks if the response is more than one word, but it is important to insure that the answer sheet has adequate space to write answers.

All subject matter included in a given controlled completion item should be related, and there should be no fewer than five or six or more than fifteen blanks in any one series. When constructing controlled completion items, make sure that the selection of the correct response for each blank depends upon knowledge of the subject matter in question. The best way to check this is to have the item answered by a person who is not familiar with the subject matter. If they can answer the questions by grammatical clues or by a process of elimination, use a different type of item.

LISTING, OR ENUMERATION, ITEMS

The listing, or enumeration, item requires the students to supply a list of terms, rules, factors, or steps that have been taught and emphasized in a given course as in Figure 8–12. The student may or may not be required to list in a particular order the responses called for. These items are used frequently but are often abused, such as when students are required to list trivial items or to memorize information that in an actual work situation could be easily found in reference material.

Each enumeration question or item should require no more than six or eight responses. When scoring, allow one point for each thing to be listed. The completion item can be modified or adapted in a variety of other ways. Cause-and-effect items can be devised so that the students supply one or the other. Generalizations can be given, with the students required to supply examples. Suggestions and associations, comparisons, and tabulations are a few of the variations that might be useful in certain situations.

CONSTRUCTING COMPLETION ITEMS

Several rules for constructing completion items will capitalize on the advantages of these recall-type items and minimize their limitations.

List in correct order the five steps to be taken in administering cardiopulmonary resuscitation (CPR).

1. _____
2. _____
3. _____
4. _____
5. _____

List the four pieces of equipment necessary to take a patient's vital signs.

6. _____
7. _____
8. _____
9. _____

FIGURE 8–12   **Enumeration Items**

Use Direct Questions

Direct questions (see Figure 8–3) will help in avoiding ambiguous statements and are less likely to contain irrelevant clues. As a general rule, items constructed using the question form will be easier to score.

Make Sentence-Completion Items Specific

State the problem or describe the situation clearly and concisely, omitting only key words; no more than two or three in a given sentence. A short statement with one key word omitted is preferable (see Figure 8–4).

Avoid Verbatim Statements

Copying statements directly from textbooks is a common fault that results in an artificial type of learning by the students in that it places undue emphasis upon rote memorization. When statements are copied verbatim, they are very likely to be ambiguous or to contain clues that give the item away. In an effort to get rid of such clues there is a tendency to leave too many blanks, with the result that the value of the item is lost entirely.

Place the Blanks at or Near the End

Placing the blank spaces at the end of the statement will provide for continuity in reading the statement and make the item more functional and logical. If the blanks come at the beginning of the item, the students must begin with a blank, read the item, and then mentally retrace their steps to decide or record what should be in the blanks. Most items of this type can be revised so that the blanks come at or near the end.

Avoid Irrelevant Clues or Distractors

Be careful that the item does not provide so much information that it can be answered solely on the basis of general intelligence. Watch out for words such as *a* and *an* when they come just before the omitted word, as they might provide a clue to the correct response. It is a poor practice to omit verbs.

Specify if More than One Correct Response Is Possible

If synonyms are to be accepted, allowing for more than one correct response, indicate this fact in the key. This suggestion pertains primarily to the simple and sentence-completion types of items. Sometimes more than one correct response may be possible for listing items, in which case it may be best to use another type of item in order to obtain objectivity in the scoring.

Call for Specific Facts

Each thing to be listed in enumeration items should involve only a few words. The students should not be required to list long, involved statements because the scoring becomes subjective.

Predetermine Scoring Order and Method

If the students are required to list responses in a given order, determine, before the test is given, how the items are to be scored. Use a system of scoring that will take off points in accordance with the number of errors made. The logic of this suggestion can be shown by considering an oversimplified "listing item" requiring the student to list the first six letters of the alphabet in correct order. Suppose the student listed them as follows: B, C, D, E, F, A, and you had placed your scoring key next to the item. How would you score the item? Would you allow no credit, or would you take off one point or two points? Note that a scoring key would not agree with any of the letters listed; yet, except for A, they follow each other in the correct order. This same problem could exist in listing any similar situation.

Many teachers would be inclined to give the student no credit if a single error is made. With respect to the alphabet this might be justified, but in doing so, it means that all students who make errors, regardless of their number, are placed in the same category. Thus the student who gets only one item out of order receives no more credit than the student who gets six out of order. There are several ways in which this might be corrected. One method is to allow one point for placing the first item first. Then allow one additional point for each item that is placed immediately after the item that it should follow.

In the alphabet example this would mean that the student would receive four points for the item. The nature of the subject matter and the objective being measured should determine the method of scoring that is followed. This is a matter to be decided by the test maker but it should be determined before the test is given.

Use Clear Illustrations

Make all sketches or illustrations clear and of sufficient size. For items in such fields as dental assisting, X-ray technology, instrument repair, and drafting, this rule is especially important.

Require Problem Solving

Whenever possible, require the students to solve problems or use previous learning. If this suggestion was followed conscientiously, it might mean that many simple and sentence-completion items would be discarded, a practice that would result in improvement in most tests. It does not mean that the common completion types should be discarded entirely, but that they should be used prudently and not be overemphasized. Completion items can be devised so that they require the student to make application of things learned. The typical teacher-made test could accommodate many more such items.

Allow Sufficient Room for Responses

As the items are being constructed, keep in mind the method that is to be used in scoring the items. Wherever possible, arrange the space for responses on one side of the page, preferably the left side, as this makes for ease of scoring. Most of the examples shown in the figures in this chapter are arranged in this manner. A better practice yet is to use a separate answer sheet.

SUMMARY

In completion items the student supplies the answer. There are various kinds and types of completion items, including simple completion, sentence completion, problems or situations, identification, and listing or enumeration.

Calvin and Hobbes

by Bill Watterson

Completion items are useful in measuring the retention of special points and are relatively easy to construct. Variations of completion items can be used effectively in obtaining a wide sampling of the subject, and they tend to have a high discriminating value.

Simple completion items are easy to construct and therefore tend to be used excessively, which then results in an overemphasis on memorization and verbal facility. Care must be exercised if subjectivity in scoring is to be avoided. The following points will be helpful in constructing completion items:

1. Use direct questions whenever possible.
2. Make sentence-completion items as specific as possible.
3. Do not copy statements directly from textbooks.
4. In simple and sentence-completion items, place the blanks at or near the end of the statement.
5. Avoid including irrelevant clues or distractors.
6. Construct the item so there is only one correct response.
7. Design enumeration items to call for specific facts.
8. One question should not call for more than six or eight things to be listed.
9. If the students are required to list things in a given order, determine before the test is given how the responses are to be scored.
10. Make all sketches or illustrations clear and of sufficient size.
11. Whenever possible, require the students to solve problems or use previous learning.
12. Be sure there is plenty of room to indicate responses.

DISCUSSION QUESTIONS

1. What have you liked or disliked about the completion items that you have been called upon to answer?

2. What are some points that must be kept in mind in using or developing illustrations for completion items?

3. What is the best method for scoring completion items of the correct-order type?

4. What generalizations can you make about recall items?

5. What are the advantages of using the actual objects in a test situation, as contrasted with pictures, symbols, or word descriptions? What are the disadvantages?

EXERCISES

1. What are some specific examples of subject matter that should be measured by completion items in your subject area?

2. Provide examples, from the subject area that you are now teaching or will teach, in which good illustrations will help to make recall items more effective.

3. Following the rules enumerated and illustrated in this chapter, create twenty-five completion items for a unit of instruction in your subject area. Five of the items should be of the "answer a question" type (Figure 8–3), five of the sentence-completion type (Figure 8–4), five of the situation completion type (Figure 8–6), five using a drawing or sketch (Figure 8–9), and five of the enumeration type (Figure 8–12). If you absolutely cannot come up with new items, you may use a maximum of five items again in a different format. Include instructions to the student for each type of item, and an answer sheet.

▶ 9

Constructing
Matching Items

Matching items require the students to match two sets of material in accordance with directions provided for each item. Common matching items consist of two columns of words or phrases. The first column is numbered to correspond to numbers of the test item, and the second column is lettered. Students are required to match each item in one list with the item in the other list to which it is most closely related. Matching items are similar in concept to multiple-choice items where the same choices are applicable in answering each of the items. They are most similar in format to controlled completion items. Matching items measure at least to the recognition level of the cognitive domain.

ADVANTAGES OF MATCHING ITEMS

Matching items may require the student to match such things as: (1) terms or words to their definitions; (2) characteristics to the mechanical units to which they apply; (3) short questions to their answers; (4) symbols to their proper names; (5) descriptive phrases to other phrases; (6) causes to effects; (7) principles to situations in which the principles apply; (8) parts or mechanical units to their proper names; (9) parts to the unit to which they belong; and (10) problems to their solutions.

The matching item is especially applicable for measuring the student's ability to recognize relationships, discriminate between concepts, classify objects according to degree of presence of a characteristic, make associations, and name and identify things learned (the who, what, where, and when type of subject matter).

Matching items are relatively easy to construct, they can be made totally objective, and they can be scored quickly. A large number of responses can be included in a small space with one group of directions. When properly constructed, the guessing factor is practically eliminated in matching items.

LIMITATIONS OF MATCHING ITEMS

The matching item provides a poor measure of complete understanding and interpretations because the phrases or clauses must be short. When compared to the multiple-choice item in measuring judgment and application of material taught, the matching item is inferior.

Matching items are likely to contain subtle clues to the correct response. Such clues are usually unintentional and therefore difficult for the test maker to detect. Using too many matching items will result in a test overemphasizing the memorization of facts. Matching items are often used—even when another type of test would provide a more valid measurement—solely because they are easy to construct.

VARIATIONS OF MATCHING ITEMS

There are numerous variations of the matching-type item. The following examples illustrate several varieties, but keep in mind that still other adaptations can be made to suit individual purposes. Each example has a sample set of directions to the student. The items in each example are numbered, beginning with one. Unlike the examples provided in previous chapters, each example provided in this chapter constitutes an entire item.

Notice that in Figures 9–1 and 9–2 the number of items in the letter column exceeds the number of items in the numbered column, in order to minimize the effect of the students completing the items they know and then being able to answer the remaining through a process of elimination, or just by guessing.

By using computer graphics programs or photocopy technology it is very easy to include illustrations in matching items, such as those shown in Figures 9–5 and 9–6. If a picture or diagram of a computer keyboard with lettered keys were shown as the lettered column (B) of Figure 9–3, it might be more realistic for the students than the list that is divorced from the actual practice of using the keyboard to perform the tasks in the numbered column. The item shown in Figure 9–4 requires the students to select a solution to the problem or situation indicated in the first column.

CONSTRUCTING MATCHING ITEMS

Determine Number of Responses

Have at least five and not more than twelve responses in each matching exercise. This is somewhat of an arbitrary rule based more on common sense and experience than research evidence. Others believe that five to seven responses are preferable.

Directions: Common medical instruments and their uses are listed in the two columns below. In the blank space at the left, place the letter identifying the instrument used to perform each operation. Use each letter only once.

_____	1. "No touch technique" surgical dressing	A. Foley catheter
_____	2. Grasp muscle or skin surrounding wounds	B. Goniometer
_____	3. Hold surgical drapes in place	C. Green autoclave
_____	4. Clamp blood vessels and hold tissue	D. Hemostatic forceps
_____	5. Grasp suture needle	E. Micro sterilizer
_____	6. Grasp foreign bodies	F. Needle holder
_____	7. Examine for auscultation	G. Sphygmomanometer
		H. Splinter forceps
		I. Sterilizer forceps
		J. Towel forceps

FIGURE 9–1 **Matching Tools or Instruments to Their Uses**

Directions: The two columns below contain terms and definitions pertaining to photocopier technology. Match each definition in Column A with the proper term in Column B. Place the indentifying letter of the term in the blank space provided.

Column A | Column B

1. _____ Amount of room between the developer sleeve and drum — A. CEL

2. _____ Reduces the charge potential on drum and aids in separation — B. DSD

3. _____ Eliminates charge in nonimage areas — C. electrical charge

4. _____ Pulls the toner from the drum to the paper — D. exposure

5. _____ Vibrates to indicate an "add toner" condition — E. PCL lamp

6. _____ Neutralizes the charge on the drum that causes the paper to fall — F. piezo element

G. photo-conductor

H. PTL

I. separation corona

J. transfer corona

FIGURE 9–2 **Terms and Their Definitions**

Directions: The two columns below contain verbal descriptions of functions performed by certain keys when using XYZ software. Match the verbal descriptions in Column A with the key indicated in Column B. Place the identifying letter in the numbered blank space at the left. Some keys may be used more than once.

Column A   Column B

1. _____ Erases the contents of a cell   A. F1
2. _____ Displays help screen   B. F2
3. _____ Makes the entry left justified   C. F3
4. _____ Erases entire worksheet   D. F4
5. _____ Displays the menu   E. F5
6. _____ Switches to edit mode   F. ESC
7. _____ Cancels a function   G. /WEY
8. _____ Indicates default for column width H. CTRL and Break
9. _____ Saves worksheet to disk   I. /
10. _____ Centers the entry   J. '
                                              K. /FS
                                              L. CTRL and C

FIGURE 9–3   **Identification of Function**

Directions: Column A below contains several accounting transactions that need a specific statement in order to record the transaction. Column B contains the names of several accounting statements. Select the statement that is needed to complete each of the transactions and place the indentifying letter in the blank space provided. Use any statement more than once if necessary.

_____ 1. The owner bought equipment by   A. Balance Sheet
           paying cash.   B. Combined Journal
_____ 2. You need to make a closing   C. Income Statement
           entry for the revenue accounts.   D. T-Account
_____ 3. You need to make a closing   E. Statement of Owner's
           entry for the expense accounts.   Equity
_____ 4. The owner invested cash in the   F. Worksheet
           business.
_____ 5. A correction has to be made to an
           Equipment Depreciation Account.

FIGURE 9–4   **Problem and Solution**

Directions: Column A below contains components of character construction used in desktop publishing. Column B displays a number of characters. Match the character from Column B with the component from Column A and place the indentifying letter in the blank space provided.

Column A   Column B

_____ 1. Ascender   V —Ⓐ   y
_____ 2. Stroke   —Ⓖ
_____ 3. Serif   d —Ⓑ   S —Ⓗ
                          b —Ⓒ
_____ 4. Shoulder   m —Ⓓ   t
_____ 5. Stern   N —Ⓔ   —Ⓘ
_____ 6. Vertex   Q —Ⓕ   P
_____ 7. Stress   —Ⓙ
                                   L —Ⓚ

FIGURE 9–5   **Identification with Illustrations**

When there are fewer than five responses, the material can usually be measured more effectively by multiple-choice items. When there are more than twelve responses, the matching item tends to become confusing and the student wastes time by having to review too many possible choices. Figure 9–6 contains a list of twenty-one items to be matched to fourteen structural parts. This example is stretching the rule just mentioned nearly to the breaking point, but it can be justified on the grounds that all items are directly related to one unit of instruction, in this case framing.

If a matching item is created with fifteen or twenty responses and no illustration (as in Figure 9–7), there are two options. First, the test writer can decide that eight or ten of the responses are adequate to sample the points in question, and shorten the item. By cutting out the obvious and weak responses, the item is usually improved. Second, two separate items with eight or ten responses in each can be created. Usually the same directions can be used for both sets. As a result of this approach the student is able to complete the two short sets in a shorter time than it takes to finish one long set.

For certain types of classification items, more than twelve responses may be justified. If the students have to keep in mind only three or four categories each time, they will be able to answer fifteen or twenty responses without too much difficulty. But, before adding long items of this type to tests, ask whether they will increase or decrease the validity of the test. Exceptional items can be justified to prove that they are really measuring what they are supposed to measure.

Include Extra Choices

Whenever possible, include at least three extra choices from which responses must be chosen. This practice will reduce the possibility of guessing or answering the

Directions: The illustration below shows a wood frame construction building. Each of the structural members is indicated with a number. A list of structural parts is provided below the drawing. Match the letter of the structural part with the numbered part on the illustration and place the letter of the part in the appropriate space on your answer sheet.

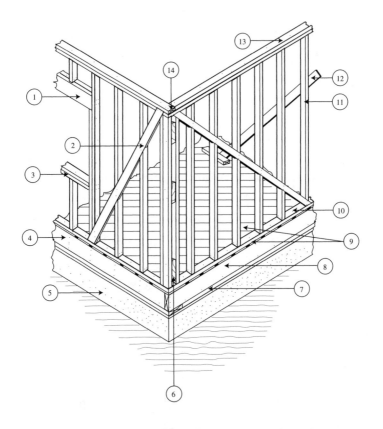

A. anchor bolt	H. joist hanger	O. stud
B. beam	I. lap plates	P. top plate
C. cleat	J. let-in brace	Q. tail joist
D. double header	K. sill plate	R. temporary brace
E. foundation	L. sole plate	S. vapor barrier
F. header joist	M. spacer block	T. window header
G. insulation	N. stringer joist	U. window sill

FIGURE 9–6   **Identification with Illustration—Separate Answer Sheet**

Directions: Several numbered questions follow. From the list provided, select the type of instrument or technique that would best be used to obtain the answer to each of those questions. Instruments or techniques may be used more than once. Place the letter of the response in the appropriate place on your answer sheet.

    A. Check of anecdotal records

    B. Interview or questionnaire

    C. Objective tests

    D. Personal observation

    E. Performance examination

1. Did all students who started the program finish?
2. Are the students ready to progress to the next unit of instruction?
3. Are employers satisfied with the technical skills of the graduates?
4. Have students' attitudes changed noticeably since the beginning of the program?
5. What was the average reading level of students at the beginning of the program?
6. How many graduates are working in the occupation six months after graduation?
7. Are the necessary equipment and supplies available to operate the class?
8. How much progress toward cognitive domain objectives has been made?
9. Are the students motivated or challenged by the program?
10. How many students are able to demonstrate appropriate skill in psychomotor domain objectives?
11. Is the program being implemented according to plan?
12. Are program graduates satisfied with the skills and knowledges they gained?

FIGURE 9–7　**Identification without Illustrations**

items by process of elimination. The several examples on the previous pages and those shown in Figures 9–8 and 9–9 illustrate this suggestion. The same results are obtained if the several choices can be used more than once, as in Figure 9–10 and in the classification type shown in Figures 9–11 and 9–12.

Use Related Materials

In any one matching item, use only materials that are related. When unrelated materials are included, the correct responses can often be determined by rationalization or process of elimination. Confine the entire matching item to one area of instruction. All the responses should be applicable to that area. Following this suggestion will remove doubts about the homogeneity of the material.

Directions: On the left list below are several types of matching test items. On the right are several types of learning. For each type of matching item on the left put the number that corresponds to that type of learning the matching item will best measure. The first item is answered as an example.

Matching Item	Type of Learning
_B_ 1. Dates with events	A. Application
_____ 2. Cause with effect	B. Association
_____ 3. Familiar problems with solutions	C. Computation skill
_____ 4. Theoretical problems with solutions	D. Following directions
	E. Judgment
_____ 5. Fractions with decimal equivalents	F. Mechanical skill
	G. Social skill
_____ 6. Terms with definitions	H. Understanding

FIGURE 9-8   **Problem Solving**

Directions: The two columns below contain illustrations of symbols used in statistics and their proper names. Match each name in the left-hand column with the proper symbol in the right-hand column. Use each symbol only once.

Column A	Column B
_____ 1. Summation	A. s'
_____ 2. Frequency	B. Σ
_____ 3. Mean	C. M
_____ 4. Standard Deviation	D. X
_____ 5. Score	E. f
_____ 6. Deviation Score	F. x
	G. LL
	H. !
	I. '

FIGURE 9-9   **Symbols and Their Names**

Directions: Which factors of a good test, listed as A, B, C, D, and E below, are implied or referred to in the eleven statements that follow? In the blank before each statement, place the letter of the term that most closely matches the message implied or referred to by the speaker.

A. Reliability
B. Validity
C. Objectivity
D. Comprehensiveness
E. Discrimination

_____ 1. "When you plan to make a test, remember that you should sample the course of study the way you would sample a restaurant."

_____ 2. "Well, I've finally finished making this test and it contains questions from all levels of difficulty."

_____ 3. "Mr. Smith, when you correct this test be sure to follow the key I made out, for the key is the only fair judge of all the students."

_____ 4. "Monica, you have taken this test three times and you have missed the same questions every time."

_____ 5. "I wonder if this test will really tell me what the students know about the subject."

_____ 6. "What is wrong with these students? I gave them a test yesterday and they did fine; today by mistake I gave them the same test and they did poorly."

_____ 7. "Although I gave the students many tests in this course and they all did very well, they still don't really know the subject matter of the course."

_____ 8. "This is the tenth time I've had to explain what the word chaos means during the test. I'd better think of a better word to used in that question."

_____ 9. "I want each item in this test to tell me exactly which students know the material and which ones don't."

_____ 10. "I have gone through the subject matter of this unit and found that thirty questions cover the unit completely."

_____ 11. "I have made each item in this test simple, concise, and to the point so anyone who knows the subject shouldn't have any trouble understanding the questions.

FIGURE 9–10 **Discrimination from a Statement**

Directions: Classify each of the following software procedures according to the five
classifications listed beneath. The first item, "decimal tabs," would be classified as a
data processing item, so an "A" is placed in the blank space before the item. Follow a
similar procedure for each item.

    A. Data processing
    B. Word processing
    C. Desktop publishing
    D. Hard disk management
    E. Disk Operating System (DOS)

__A__	1. decimal tabs		_____	9. creating art files
_____	2. comparison operators		_____	10. creating subdirectories
_____	3. floppy disk formatting		_____	11. pica settings
_____	4. partitioning a disk		_____	12. multilevel sorting
_____	5. creating batch files		_____	13. using a mouse
_____	6. importing graphics		_____	14. creating drives
_____	7. arithmetic operators		_____	15. running checkdisk
_____	8. elite settings		_____	16. creating graphs

FIGURE 9–11   **Classification of Items**

Place Long Statements on Left

Whenever possible, place the column containing the longer statements on the left
side of the page. Require the students to record their responses at the left of this column or on a separate answer sheet. If this practice is followed, then as the students
select a response, they only have to glance over the single words at the right, rather
than reading through the longer statements. This saves time and makes the process of
selection easier for the students. It also makes it easier to score when scoring is done
by hand.

Use Illustrations When Possible

This suggestion is especially applicable to matching items pertaining to tools, parts,
mechanical units, and the like. Descriptions and definitions of such things are often
confusing to the students, even though they may know the points being tested. Simple drawings will usually correct the confusion and save time in answering. Adver-
tising brochures, government publications, dictionaries, other text material, and
computer graphics programs are ideal sources for illustrations to use in matching

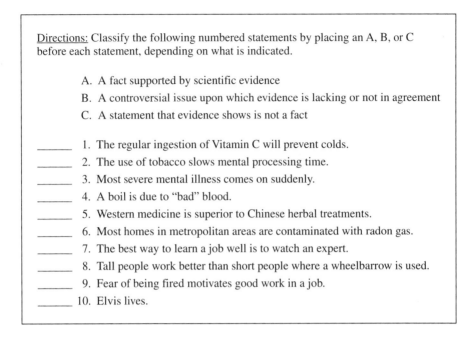

Directions: Classify the following numbered statements by placing an A, B, or C before each statement, depending on what is indicated.

    A. A fact supported by scientific evidence

    B. A controversial issue upon which evidence is lacking or not in agreement

    C. A statement that evidence shows is not a fact

_____ 1. The regular ingestion of Vitamin C will prevent colds.

_____ 2. The use of tobacco slows mental processing time.

_____ 3. Most severe mental illness comes on suddenly.

_____ 4. A boil is due to "bad" blood.

_____ 5. Western medicine is superior to Chinese herbal treatments.

_____ 6. Most homes in metropolitan areas are contaminated with radon gas.

_____ 7. The best way to learn a job well is to watch an expert.

_____ 8. Tall people work better than short people where a wheelbarrow is used.

_____ 9. Fear of being fired motivates good work in a job.

_____ 10. Elvis lives.

FIGURE 9–12   **More Classification**

items. Photocopying machines make the inclusion of illustrations easy and the items fun to construct.

Use Logical Order

Arrange the selection column in a logical order so it is easier for the students to locate the correct responses. The selection column will usually be on the right side, although in classification items and other modifications it may be in another place.

When the column consists of a series of words, these should be placed in alphabetical order. A series of numbers or dates should be placed in ascending or descending order. Placing the responses in a haphazard order causes the typical reader to be confused, at least as they start out to try to answer the item, because the random order will force them to look back and forth and up and down.

Remember the Student

Keep the student in mind as the items are prepared. Try to determine the lines of reasoning the students will follow as they look at the item. Think of all the possible ways each response might be answered. This will usually result in some changes and improvements, and is also a helpful way of locating ambiguous choices and irrelevant clues.

Everything on One Page

Make sure the entire exercise or item appears on one page. It is disconcerting, to say the least, when some of the choices are on one side of the test paper and the remainder on the other side. (This rule also applies to the construction of multiple-choice items.) The test maker should check carefully to make certain this is carried out properly if the test is typed and reproduced by someone else.

Make the Directions Specific

This is another general rule that applies to the construction of all kinds of items. State the area of instructions to which the things listed apply. Tell how the matching is to proceed. Be sure to emphasize how many times the choices may be used. The directions accompanying the figures in this chapter will serve as useful guides.

Use Capital Letters

Use upper-case (capital) letters to label the parts in the column from which responses are to be selected. This suggestion will result in more legible student-written responses, since the differences among capital letters are more pronounced than among lower-case letters.

SUMMARY

Matching items require the matching of two sets of materials in accordance with given directions. In a sense they are a variation of the multiple-choice item. They are especially applicable for measuring the who, what, where, and when type of subject matter. They are relatively easy to construct, can be made objective, and can be scored quickly.

The typical matching item provides a poor indication of complete understanding and is inferior to the multiple-choice item for measuring judgment and application. It is apt to stress the memorization of facts and will often contain subtle, irrelevant clues to the correct response.

DISCUSSION QUESTIONS

1. A matching item is a variation of the multiple-choice item. When should each type be used? What is the advantage of each?

2. Do you prefer a matching or identification-type item? Why?

3. What is the difference between the classification type and a regular matching item?

4. Why is it a poor policy to include more than twelve responses in a single matching exercise?

5. Explain why a classification item might include more than twelve responses.

6. Explain why the length of responses makes a difference as to the placement of columns.

7. Explain what is meant by homogeneous materials. Use examples from your particular field of interest.

8. Why should one column contain more items than the other?

EXERCISES

1. Prepare a matching item made up of short questions and their answers.

2. Prepare a matching item for your subject in which the students are required to match terms area to their definitions (see Figure 9–2).

3. Prepare a matching item for your subject area in which the students are required to match problems to solutions (see Figure 9–4).

4. Prepare a matching item for your subject area that uses an illustration, such as a picture of a machine, a tool, or the like (see Figure 9–6).

5. Prepare a matching item in which the students are required to identify items or conditions from verbal descriptions (see Figure 9–7).

6. Prepare a matching item that requires the student to discriminate something on the basis of a statement (see Figure 9–10).

7. Prepare a matching item that requires students to classify items or behavior (see Figure 9–11).

8. Many matching items can easily be made into simple recall items, such as completion items. Prepare a sample of this process.

▶ 10

Constructing Essay Items

Essay test items require the students to make a comparison, write a description, or explain certain points on which instruction has been given. People do not usually think of essay items as objective items in the same sense as true-false and multiple-choice items, but in reality a well-constructed essay item can be made objective in nature. Like completion items, essay questions are a type of recall item. It is difficult to state explicitly where simple completion items requiring only recall stop and essay items begin, but the emphasis on most essay items is on organization of a subject, relationships, application of principles and knowledge to new areas, synthesis, and evaluation. Some essay items are posed as questions, while others are of a situational type requiring comparison, discussion, or explanation.

Although criticism is often leveled against them, essay items can and should be used effectively to assess student performance. They have value in measuring the ability of the students to organize their thoughts and to express themselves clearly. They can be devised to measure ability and understanding in a wide variety of subject areas.

For the purpose intended here, the essay item is considered the type in which the student is allowed freedom of expression in describing, explaining, comparing, or reasoning. This is in contrast to completion items (see Chapter 8) that require the student merely to list, enumerate, or name something, and in which the responses are "forced," and require a specific word or phrase response. Essay items, then, are considered another of the various types of test items used to measure mastery of certain kinds of learning.

ADVANTAGES AND LIMITATIONS OF ESSAY ITEMS

Essay questions or items are not particularly suitable for use in assessing subject areas in which the final behavior consists primarily of physical manipulation of

"The subject was inexplicable, so I didn't try to explick it."

© Martha F. Campbell

objects, tools, or materials. This is because they place a premium on students' abilities to express themselves in writing, rather than on their abilities to apply practically the knowledge or skills that have been taught. If students will be required to write reports or descriptions on the job, the essay examination is one way of determining their ability to do so. Examples of occupations that require such activities include nursing, police work, construction estimation, and insurance adjusting.

Essay items often have low reliability because of the narrow sampling of the subject area. There is also low reliability in the marking or scoring. A good answer read after a so-so one will be rated as excellent, while the same answer read after an excellent answer will be rated as poor or so-so. The main disadvantage of essay examinations, then, is that they are hard to grade objectively. They are also time-consuming to correct, and their use may encourage bluffing. These disadvantages can be overcome by asking for specific information by establishing a rubric, or a set of guidelines that can be written in a short paragraph. The basis of the answer, or a prompt, should be given. This is particularly true in questions where the students are asked to discuss something. An example of an answer prompt is given in the section below that discusses the rules for constructing essay tests.

Low validity is also a problem with essay items. It has been said that not only do essay items often not measure what they purport to, but they take longer *not* to do it.

Essay items may be comprehensive in nature, and as such, will be difficult to fit readily into a typical teacher-made test. In other words, it is not usually possible to have the students organize their thoughts and express themselves completely in two or five or ten minutes, as is necessary in the ordinary test. The ability to work independently, to locate sources of material, and to organize a presentation are also highly important outcomes of effective learning. They cannot be measured by true-false and similar items, and they cannot be measured readily by requiring the students to close their books and react to a group of stereotyped items.

It is possible when using essay items to allow the students to examine a quantity of materials before organizing and expressing their thoughts. Students might be given a week or more to prepare their replies. This procedure begins to approach the term-paper assignment except that it is more restricted and is based on the suggestions that follow for the construction and correction of essay items. The paper would be prepared and scored in accordance with careful, predetermined specifications. Essay items of this type would, in most instances, be used very sparingly because of the time involved with their preparation and scoring. Such items do eliminate reading and writing speed as factors that determine success in answer preparation.

VARIATIONS OF ESSAY ITEMS

There are a number of types of essay questions, or rather there are a number of different kinds of learning that can be measured with essay questions. Some of those that are appropriate to occupational subjects are illustrated in the figures that follow. The examples are all from different subject areas. Additional examples may be found in the discussion questions at the end of the chapter.

The first type of essay item requests the students to compare two things, either on a single basis or in general (see Figure 10–1). This is the lowest level of learning measured by an essay question.

Comparison on Single Basis.

    Compare fuel injection and carburation systems on the basis of fuel economy.

Comparison in General.

    Compare fuel injection and carburation systems.

Note: Be sure to provide enough space to answer the question.

FIGURE 10–1 **Comparison**

The question shown in Figure 10–2 requires the students to make decisions for or against something and to support their answers. This kind of question requires a greater depth of thinking and reasoning than the issue shown in Figure 10–1.

In your opinion, should students in occupational education programs be taught to the first, second, or third level of learning? Why?

FIGURE 10–2   **Decision for or against**

Figure 10–3 presents an essay question that requires the students not only to recall data, but also to analyze the impact of those events or data. This is a higher level cognitive domain behavior and approaches the "qualified" level of the three-level classification system discussed in Chapter 2.

How do you account for the dramatic decline in number of dental caries in preteen children in the last twenty years?

FIGURE 10–3   **Cause or Effects**

Another form of essay question requires the student to restate or explain a passage or statement (see Figure 10–4). This type of question is particularly useful in occupational education to determine the level of understanding of legislation, regulations, or specifications. This is lower-level cognitive or affective domain performance.

The licensure law for barbers and cosmetologists states: ". . ." What does this mean for the practicing barber or cosmetologist?

FIGURE 10–4   **Explanation**

Essay items may also be used as a teaching device to reinforce learning by having the students summarize a unit of instruction or textual material (see Figure 10–5). When using this kind of item, be sure that the students do not just memorize the material and parrot back the same words or phrases without having developed any understanding of the concepts being tested.

Summarize in not more than one page the argument for smog testing by state-certified stations only.

FIGURE 10–5   **Summary**

Yet another type of essay item requires the learner to analyze the reasons for some phenomenon (see Figure 10–6). The word *analyze* does not have to be part of the question, but the behavior required of the student should be analysis.

Why do the teacher preparation requirements for vocational teachers differ from those for "academic" teachers?

FIGURE 10–6   **Analysis**

A seventh type of essay item (see Figure 10–7) asks the student to describe relationships between elements of the subject they are learning. This is a low- to middle-level cognitive domain performance.

Describe the relationship between type size, type style, and line leading in typesetting.

FIGURE 10–7   **Describe Relationships**

One of the highest forms of learning is when students can generalize what they have learned to new situations. Essay items can be used to determine the ability to apply rules or principles to new situations, or can test at least the knowledge of such rules or principles. The item in Figure 10–8 requires the student to extrapolate from one situation with certain circumstances to another situation with similar circumstances.

Given the results of the basic skills testing requirements for teachers in California, what do you expect to be the effect of the same requirements in New York?

FIGURE 10–8   **Application of Rules**

Another type of essay item asks the student to discuss a topic (see Figure 10–9). This is a rather broad way of determining knowledge, so the instructor is advised to be somewhat specific (restrictive) in what is to be discussed.

In the space below, discuss how enzymes work by tracing the action that takes place. Use a drawing if necessary to support your written answer.

FIGURE 10–9   **Discuss**

Essay items may also be used to have students express the relevance of statements or criticism of their accuracy. They can be used to require students to outline procedures or to reorganize facts. Essay items can even be used to have students create new questions and procedures from existing knowledge. In most instances, essay questions can be used to determine learning at advanced stages of instruction, that is, that portion of the subject that is to be learned to the third level.

CONSTRUCTING ESSAY ITEMS

As in any other item, it is first necessary to decide upon the objective to be measured and then write down exactly what you want to measure. For example, you might want to determine whether the students understand how an enzyme actually works. Conceivably this could be measured by using other types of items (cluster true-false or several multiple-choice). In this instance, the objective, or purpose, is to find out how well the students can use their own words to describe what happens and a short essay item would work better than the other types. Do not include a question until its purpose has been clearly defined.

The second rule is to call for specific answers. Do not use items that require the students to write all that they know about a particular topic. State the item in a simple, direct manner. Word the statement in such a way as to provide the students with an outline they can follow in formulating their responses.

Poor

What is the difference between an apple and an orange?

Better

Compare an apple with an orange in terms of nutritional value, calories, and taste. Your response will be scored by allowing one point for each significant item related to the three criteria. A total of 15 points may be earned for correctly responding to this item.

Essay items should be worded so as to restrict (or guide) the response toward the objective it is desired to measure.

Essay items should require the students to compare, explain why, describe, or tell how. Having the students list or enumerate some process or procedure can be accomplished with completion items, so use the simpler type of item to determine this type of knowledge. Requiring comparison or explanation will ensure an item that calls for application of concepts or materials learned.

Before administering an essay examination, determine definite specifications for marking or scoring the responses. For example, allow one point for each significant point expected in the response. This, rather than the assumed importance of the item, should form the basis for weighting or assigning a value to it. The best practice is to write out the points that are to be covered in the item and use them as a checklist when marking the responses.

Some essay items cannot be scored as readily as this because the specific points to be covered are not always so apparent, or there is a wide variety of possible answers. These conditions should be noted as the item is constructed. Often a few changes in the directions will make possible more objective scoring.

When marking or scoring essay items, follow a definite procedure. It should be readily apparent that the method of scoring essay items is an important factor affecting their validity. The first step of scoring is to write out the answer expected for each item, including all points that are to be accepted. It is impractical to do this *only* on those occasions when you know everything there is to know about the subject and the ways in which your students will answer. Second, score one essay item on all test papers before proceeding to the next.

The third step of the scoring procedure is to give specific values to an item by allowing one point for each point covered in the answer. Fourth, in order to "depersonalize" the scoring process, conceal the students' names on the test papers, or in some manner make sure their identity is not revealed as the item is being scored.

It is a matter of teacher judgment whether to use essay items with other types in a single test. There will be instances where essay items can be used effectively right along with multiple-choice, matching, and other types of items. In these cases they will likely be of the short-answer variety and hard to distinguish from completion items.

SUMMARY

Essay items require the students to make a comparison, write a description, or explain certain points. The students are allowed freedom of expression in analyzing, comparing, describing, explaining, or reasoning. Essay items are especially useful in occupational education in those subjects or occupations where employees are required to write reports or perform written activities on the job .

It is easy to criticize and ridicule the essay tests sometimes used by teachers that require students to write everything they know about a subject—and do it within a fifty-minute class period! The subjectivity of the scoring, the poor sampling of what has been learned, the amount of time necessary to answer only a few questions, and the opportunity for bluffing on the part of the student have all been major points of condemnation of the essay examination. Unfortunately, essay items themselves have been condemned, rather than the method by which they were constructed, used, and scored. In other words, essay items are not inherently inferior. They can provide very useful information about students' development or achievement and should be considered carefully along with other types of items when determining the best method for measuring a particular objective.

Following are five points that will be helpful in constructing essay items:

1. Decide upon the objective to be measured. Be specific.
2. Call for specific answers.
3. Require the student to "compare," "explain why," "describe," or "tell how," not to "list," or "enumerate."
4. Determine definite specifications for marking.
5. Follow a definite procedure in scoring the papers.

DISCUSSION QUESTIONS

The first four questions concern the subject of testing and are stated in the form of essay questions. Try to determine the behavior or learning activity sought in each question.

1. Compare essay examinations and multiple-choice examinations from the standpoint of their effect upon the study procedures used by the student.

2. Compare norm-referenced and criterion-referenced tests.

3. In your opinion, should teacher-made test results have more weight than standardized test results in determining student advancement? Why?

4. How do you account for the propensity to use objective tests in the schools?

5. What factors have led to the severe decrease in vocational teacher education requirements in the last twenty years?

6. The Teacher Preparation and Licensure Law requires that all vocational teachers have a total of five years of occupational experience, with one of those years having occurred within the last three years. Why?

7. Why is it so difficult to use essay tests in occupational instruction?

8. Why is it that no matter what the subject being tested, when essay items are used they tend to be measures of the learner's mastery of English?

9. Why is it important for the teacher to write out the answer expected on essay items before the test is given?

10. Why should all students' answers to each particular essay item be read before proceeding to the next question?

11. Think back to the essay items that you have been asked to respond to (or have given to students). How did you feel about those items? Were you always sure what the teacher was looking for? How would you now improve those items?

EXERCISES

1. Select a word or term in your subject area that needs to be understood by students. Now devise an essay test item that will measure a real understanding of the word or term. Prepare an answer of the kind that you would expect.

2. Select a process followed in your subject area that students must understand and be able to follow. Devise an essay item that will determine the students' understanding of the process. *Note:* Do not simply ask the students to enumerate the process. Prepare an answer of the kind that you would expect to receive from the students.

3. Create an essay item that requires the students to analyze the reasons for some phenomenon, such as that illustrated in Figure 10–9. Provide instructions to the students as part of the item that indicates how their answers will be scored, then prepare an answer of the kind that you would expect from the students.

RESOURCES

A Reference List and Selected Bibliography

Carter, K. (1984). "Do teachers understand principles for writing tests?" *Journal of Teacher Education*, *35*, 57–60.

Hopkins, C.D., & Antes, R.L. (1990). *Classroom measurement and evaluation*, Third Edition. Itasca, IL: F.E. Peacock.

Tuchman, B.W. (1993, October). "The essay test: A look at the advantages and disadvantages," NAASP Bulletin, 77, 20–26.

▶ 11

Evaluating
Manipulative
Performance

Throughout, this book has placed emphasis upon the importance of evaluating the students' achievement in terms of objectives derived from an analysis of the needs of the subject or occupation. The necessity of sampling all aspects of student mastery has also been stressed. The development of skill in the performance of certain manipulative operations is usually one of the primary objectives for almost every occupational education course and for courses in such other programs as physical education. This means that the measurement of the students' ability to perform manipulative operations should be an important part of the total program of evaluation for such courses.

Written tests are not valid for the measurement of manipulative skills. A student's ability to supply flawless answers to questions about how to perform some skill is *not* evidence that the student can actually perform the action to any acceptable degree. It is equally true that failure to answer questions satisfactorily on a written test would *not* be an indication of one's inability to perform the skill.

In spite of the general agreement with this point of view, far too many teachers state as one of their main objectives the development of certain manipulative skills, spend the greater portion of class time in developing those skills, and then administer a few written tests as the only means of measuring subject mastery. Often, the teacher even begins keeping student progress records but discontinues entries after the first few weeks of school. The hasty placing of grades on finished projects at the end of the term does not provide an adequate measure and evaluation of manipulative skill.

PROGRESS CHARTS

There are three basic means of measuring and evaluating the students' skill in the performance of manipulative operations. One method is through careful, systematic, objective observation of the students' daily work and the recording of the results at frequent intervals on some form of *progress chart* or record. (See Figure 11–1 for an example of a typical student progress chart.) This chart, or a computerized version of it, can be used to record all student activities in a given course. Keep in mind that such a chart is only a record of the activities that are being used to document the students' progress in mastering the skills of the course; it is not in itself a measure of their progress. Never display student progress charts in a classroom or allow other students to see the entire chart unless the charts have no names and are coded in such a fashion that each student knows only his or her own code and cannot determine the code of other students. Publicly displaying student grades or scores with names or other identifying characteristics is a violation of students' privacy, and therefore a violation of the law.

CHECKLISTS

The careful checking, testing, and evaluation of finished projects or products provides a second method of measuring and evaluating student skill. Figure 11–2 is an example of a *checklist* that could be used for examination and evaluation of a finished project. This particular checklist is one that would be used to check a test maker's construction of true-false items. Such a checklist does not consider the process followed; only the final product achieved. For all the teacher knows, the students could have taken two hours to do a ten-minute job, or they could have reversed the procedure, or they could even have had someone else produce the product. On the other hand, the only thing the teacher sees is the finished product, so product evaluation could be more objective than process evaluation (described below), because standards, appearance, function, design, and accuracy are judged against prespecified standards. The problems associated with using this method as a sole assessment of a student's progress should be obvious.

PERFORMANCE TESTS

The administration of *performance tests* is a third possibility for determining the level of proficiency of students in performing manipulative skills. Occupational educators have been using performance tests for years as a primary method of evaluation. Educators from other areas have adopted the method and termed it "authentic assessment," because students are required to perform a task rather than select answers from a prepared list, as they do in most objective tests. There are several

Progress Chart

Course:______________ Instructor:______________ Location:______________

Activity Number or Date Completed																										
Possible Points																										
Activity																										
Students' Names																										
1																										
2																										
3																										
4																										
5																										
6																										
7																										
8																										
9																										
10																										
12																										
13																										
14																										
15																										
16																										
17																										
18																										
19																										
20																										
21																										
22																										
23																										
24																										
25																										
26																										
27																										
28																										
29																										
30																										
31																										
32																										

FIGURE 11–1 **A Sample Progress Chart**

True-False Test Items

The test maker's true-false items meet the following criteria:

	YES	NO
1. All statements are entirely true or entirely false.	_____	_____
2. No trivial details are used to make statements false.	_____	_____
3. The statements are clear and concise.	_____	_____
4. The statements are not verbatim from a textbook.	_____	_____
5. The statements avoid the use of specific determiners.	_____	_____
6. The statements are in positive form.	_____	_____
7. A pattern of responses is avoided in the items.	_____	_____
8. The scoring is arranged in a convenient manner.	_____	_____

COMMENTS: _____

_____

_____

LEVEL OF PERFORMANCE: All items must receive "yes" responses. "No" responses require revision or justification.

FIGURE 11–2   **Checklist for Finished Project**

types of activities used in authentic (also called alternative) assessment. Some of these activities, other than manipulative activities, will be discussed in Chapter 13. Assessment of manipulative abilities is described below and is referred to throughout as "performance" testing.

In a comprehensive program of measurement and evaluation, all three methods are used to measure manipulative skill. The remainder of this chapter is devoted to the performance test.

Advantages of Performance Tests

There are several advantages of performance tests. They can be designed and administered to provide a more objective, reliable, and valid measure of the student's ability to perform certain operations than can be obtained by any other practicable means. Also, they provide a careful analysis and measurement of the extent to which the student has mastered the various elements of skill. This is especially important from the standpoint of diagnosis and reteaching.

The results obtained by administering carefully prepared performance tests enable teachers to analyze the effectiveness of their own demonstrations and they reveal points upon which greater emphasis should be placed. Taking a performance test and studying its results lets the students analyze their own strengths and weaknesses. This experience focuses attention upon the details that make for effective performance, or the process of creating a product or project. Performance tests measure the results of instruction in their direct application, not indirectly through some mental process, and they do so while the student is actually performing or demonstrating the task.

Limitations of Performance Tests

The major limitations and difficulties of performance tests lie in their construction and administration. Even though they can be carefully constructed to yield objective and reliable measurements, the teacher who administers them must have considerable training and experience in order to obtain objective and reliable results.

The administration of performance tests consumes considerable time. One teacher can administer a performance test to between two and perhaps six students at a time. In some cases only one student can take the test at a given time with satisfactory results. Performance test administration thus presents the problem of planning profitable activities for students who are waiting to take the test and for those who have already completed it. Performance testing involves an element of what might easily be misconstrued as "busy work," something most instructors prefer to keep to a minimum in their teaching.

Though they contain a great amount of detail and objectivity, performance tests can be misleading. The fact that they require actual performance on the part of the student does not necessarily make them good tests. The formality and control that characterize the administration of performance tests tend to penalize the student who experiences difficulty in working under pressure. This limitation is minimized by replicating actual working conditions as close as possible.

The type of performance test presented in this chapter is not to be confused with the *object test,* which was covered in the chapter on completion items, or with standardized aptitude tests involving manipulative performance. The object test makes use of actual tools, materials, and equipment in measuring the student's *cognitive* knowledge of these items and their uses. There may be some performance incorporated in test situations set up at certain stations in the object test, but the performance must necessarily be limited to the completion of only one or two steps of an operation or the execution of a very simple, short procedure. Object tests may involve some elements closely related to performance, but in the main they measure knowledge and understanding.

An *aptitude test* involving manipulative performance is designed to predict the student's potential skill. The function of the test in this case is to judge either how quickly the student can develop the skills required for performance of particular job duties or the level of such skills that the student might be able to develop. Other forms of aptitude instruments test for spatial relations abilities.

The *trade test* involving performance is designed to measure efficiency in a given trade, and is used for the purpose of selection and placement of people on the job, or for promotion or reclassification purposes. The administration of a trade test may consume anywhere from several hours to two or three days. The person being tested may remain under the direct observation of the examiner during the entire period, or as is done in some instances, the examiner may merely check the completed work to determine the score on the test.

Neither the aptitude nor the trade test would provide an adequate measure of achievement in the classroom. The aptitude test would certainly be invalid for this purpose, and there would be very few cases in which a trade test, even if there were time to administer it to all students in the class, would measure manipulative achievement gained in a particular course. A series of performance tests designed for that course by the teacher is a far better measure of student achievement.

MEASURABLE ASPECTS OF PERFORMANCE

Conscious manipulative performance is a highly complex process, and its accurate measurement is likewise complicated. Before the teacher can design instruments for measuring accurately the student's ability to perform manipulative operations, it is necessary to understand the various measurable aspects of performance.

Manipulative performance is not merely a matter of physical *doing*. There is also considerable *knowing* involved, so the performance being tested is related to mental or intellectual processes. The manipulative operations to be performed constitute problems to be solved. Their solution requires physical work of a skilled order accompanied and directed by the conscious application of previously acquired knowledge and understanding. The performer is continually analyzing the problem and evaluating progress during the performance test. At practically every turn the student has to weigh technical knowledge and understanding and make certain choices and decisions that affect the work being done. In fact, the technical knowledge applied in completing the performance in many cases overshadows the actual "doing" in importance.

ESSENTIAL FEATURES OF MANIPULATIVE PERFORMANCE

Important elements of skill that should be considered in evaluating a student's ability to perform a given operation or series of related operations are described in the following paragraphs.

Speed

Speed is the student's rate of work as compared with a predetermined standard, which almost always will be set by the acceptable time to perform the skill on the job. For example, if it is necessary for a nurse on the job to be able to start an IV within two minutes, that same time standard will be applied in the performance test. Speed may be combined with other criteria, such as when firefighter trainees are required to drag a heavy inert object (simulating a body) so many feet in so many seconds.

Quality

The precision with which the student works and the extent to which the completed job conforms to prescribed dimensions and specifications constitute quality. This is often nothing more than checking dimensions, but more often it involves decisions about the appearance or texture of a product being produced.

Procedure

Procedure involves the extent to which the student follows the detailed steps of the accepted method for completing the prescribed job. It also includes the extent to which the student demonstrates the ability to select, care for, and use properly the tools, materials, and equipment required to complete the job. The observance of safety precautions and actions should always be part of the procedure. The application of essential information in making decisions affecting performance is measured, and the confidence, deliberation, and self-assurance with which the work is performed is evaluated.

The well-constructed performance test provides for the measurement of each of these important elements of skill. A test designed to measure only one of these, such as rate of work or the observance of safety precautions, is of questionable value, even though such tests are frequently given in an effort to analyze a student's specific strengths and weaknesses. A test administered to measure rate of performance without regard to the other elements of skill will cause the student to sacrifice such items as accuracy, proper procedure, and proper use and care of tools, instruments, or equipment for speed. A high level of achievement in any one aspect of skill when measured by itself is of no particular consequence. The student's skill in the performance of manipulative operations must be measured and analyzed by use of testing situations in which both examiner and student place appropriate emphasis upon *each* aspect of performance—speed, quality, and procedure.

Certain aspects of performance can be measured directly and rather objectively either while the student works or by checking and testing the completed job. Other elements may only be evaluated by more subjective action of the observer. For example, the time required to complete the various operations included in the job and the total time consumed by the entire performance can be accurately measured with a stopwatch and recorded by an observer. The observer can determine definitely that the student either did or did not do certain procedural steps and can record in an objective manner those observations. The extent to which the completed work conforms to specifications can be accurately determined by the use of precision measuring instruments. However, such items as the confidence and assurance with which the student tackled the job, the general appearance of the finished product, and the extent to which marks, scratches, imperfections, and other blemishes mar the work do not lend themselves readily to precise and objective measurement but are left to the subjective judgment of the observer.

CONSTRUCTING PERFORMANCE TESTS

A performance test is designed to analyze and measure the student's skill in the performance of selected operations under rigidly controlled conditions. As the students complete specific operations, the teacher carefully observes their performance and records on a previously prepared checklist the extent to which the standards are met. The checklist will have been developed from analyses of the tasks as they are performed on the job and from the course objectives. The time required to perform the various phases of the operation is recorded; a record is made of the precision and accuracy with which the student works; errors in procedure are noted and checked; the application and observation of specific points and safety precautions are recorded; and the completed work is carefully measured and checked. The performance test provides the basis for a thorough analysis of the entire performance and an evaluation of each element in that performance.

The construction of satisfactory performance tests is not an easy task. A careful, detailed analysis of operations to be incorporated in the test is necessary for a performance test of high quality. Considerable initiation and imagination must be exercised in order to devise means of measuring all the important aspects of student performance.

The performance test requires the student to complete one or more significant operations under rigidly controlled conditions. Each operation involves several steps, and completion of the test by the student generally requires ten to fifty minutes. The student is observed carefully during the performance, and a detailed record is made of everything done. There may be as many as thirty or forty or more items against which performance is checked.

Complete performance tests usually include directions for the test administrator, detailed descriptions of the activity to be performed by the students, directions to be followed by the students, a method of recording time used, checklists for the observers, and a final checklist or sign-off sheet.

There is no rigid, mechanical procedure that can be followed to ensure the construction of an objective, reliable, and valid, yet practical, performance test. The following general procedures, together with some specific suggestions, should prove helpful.

Select the Operations to Be Incorporated

The difficulties involved in their construction, the time required to administer performance tests, and the basic necessity of providing valid measures of achievement make it mandatory that operations to be included in the performance test be selected with care; a random selection will not suffice. When the instructor compiles the list of items that must be mastered by students if the course objectives pertaining to manipulative skill are to be realized, numerous operations will be listed for any course. The degree of efficiency achieved in certain of these operations will lend itself to measurement by performance tests. For practical reasons, the use of performance tests to measure proficiency in all of these operations should not be attempted, but test items should include interrelated tasks and duty areas as performed on the job. The following suggestions should prove helpful in selecting operations that may be satisfactorily incorporated in performance tests.

1. Operations should be typical and representative of those that have been taught.
2. By the time the test is to be administered, the operations will have been demonstrated to and practiced by all students to be tested.
3. The operations selected should be able to be completed in fifteen to fifty minutes. It is not practical to design a performance test that a given student cannot complete in one class period.
4. Operations should be sufficiently difficult to reveal any real and significant differences in achievement, yet also reveal the minimum criteria level for the objective. Operations that can be performed equally well by all students are probably not suitable for testing purposes. In order to determine degree of proficiency, it is necessary to choose deliberately those operations that, in performance, either result in perceptible errors or provide opportunities for variation in one or more of the measurable aspects of performance.
5. Operations should involve the instruments, tools, materials, and equipment commonly used in the course and the subject area field.
6. There must be sufficient sets of necessary tools and equipment to permit preparation of the number of workstations required to complete the administration of the test to the class in a reasonable length of time.
7. Operations should involve definite steps of procedure and require the application of specific knowledge and understanding along with the manipulative work.

In other words, select operations that will not overtax personnel, time, equipment, materials, and testing facilities.

Make a Preliminary Analysis of Each Operation

Until this preliminary analysis has been made, the selection of operations to include in the test must necessarily remain tentative. The analysis of each operation should reveal: (1) the approved step-by-step procedure to be followed in performing the operation, together with the specific safety precautions to be observed and the more important points of information the student must consider and apply to complete the operation satisfactorily; and (2) the tools and equipment required to perform the operation.

If the teacher makes extensive use of analysis procedures in organizing subject matter for instructional purposes (job and task analysis), this second step in the construction of a performance test will probably become one of making a careful study of the analyses already available in curriculum documents.

Select or Design an Appropriate Exercise

After the operations to be incorporated in the performance test have been analyzed, the next step is to design a simple job or exercise in which these operations, but no others, are involved. This job should be definite, specific, and one that can be completed in an acceptable length of time.

Prepare Drawings and Specifications for the Job

If the job involves construction or creation of an item or product, a working drawing should be prepared (see Figure 11–3). The drawing and specifications should leave no doubt as to what is required of the student. Further, they serve as a guide to the examiner in preparing the physical setup for the performance test, and thus become essential to the standardization of testing procedure.

List All Specific Points Feasible for Testing Purposes

This calls for a careful study of the preliminary analysis completed as the second step of the test construction and of the drawing and specifications for the job to be performed by the student, in order to arrive at a comprehensive list of the specific points from which to select those to be included in the test. A consideration of the means of measurement available will not only aid in the completion of this list but will result in a classification or grouping of the points, which will in turn facilitate the construction of the mechanical aspects of the test. While the objectives of the course will lead to the selection of the major elements to be included in the test, it is not until the test job has been designed and adequately described that the detailed points that may be included in the test can be listed and a means of measuring each systematically prescribed.

Certain aspects of the performance must necessarily be checked by an observer

This performance test is designed to measure your manipulative skills as you work in preparing and bending copper tubing.

Using the materials furnished, you will prepare and bend three pieces of tubing to the dimensions shown in the drawing below.

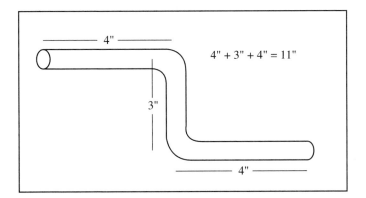

Note: All dimensions are from center to center.

USING A $^1/_4$" RIGID BENDER AND THE DIMENSIONS SHOWN:

A. Make two bends off of the 90-degree mark on your bender for the forward bend.

B. Make two 45-degree bends using the 45-degree mark on your bender and the dimensions shown above.

C. Make two 90-degree bends using the "R" mark for the reverse bend technique.

FIGURE 11–3 **Student Instructions**

as the student executes the job requirement, while other qualities can best be measured by checking the student's completed work. Under each of these classifications of points to be evaluated there will appear: (1) Certain items that can be measured objectively, either by observing that specific acts were or were not performed or by making use of precision measuring instruments to determine the degree or extent of variation from a specified standard; and (2) qualities whose measurement becomes a matter of the judgment of the examiner. In the majority of instances the measurement of qualities of the latter type will require provisions for distinguishing among varying degrees of compliance with standards or specifications.

Ordinarily, the qualities listed should be expressed in terms of effective or correct performance; however, in the case of errors commonly made, evidence that the student guarded against a given difficulty or avoided a common error may be included as a point for which credit may be given.

Select the Specific Points to Be Included

From the list of items included in the analysis, select the points against which the students' performance should be checked. Obviously, provisions for the inclusion of every specific item listed in the analysis cannot be made. After considering such factors as: (1) the relative importance and relationship of each item to competence in the performance of the operation of which it is a part, (2) the objectivity and reliability with which it can be measured, (3) its discriminating power, and (4) the availability of means for its measurement, the instructor may choose the items for the test. Only after the test has been completed and administered to several students and analyses made of the results obtained can the teacher have any better basis than personal judgment or the combined judgments of several teachers in the field for the selection of specific items for the test. (See Figure 11–4 for an example.)

Construct the Checklist

The specific items to be included in the performance test are incorporated in the checklist to be used in administering the test. The checklist will usually include two distinct sections: one to be executed by the examiner either during or immediately following the student's performance, the second to be used to record the results of a care-

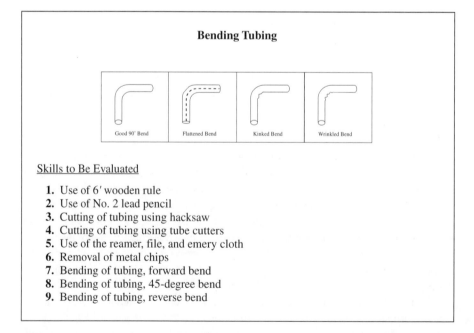

FIGURE 11–4   **Factors to Be Evaluated**

ful analysis of the student's completed work. The checklist (see Figure 11–5) is developed directly from the list of skills to be evaluated (see Figure 11–4). Following are some points to observe when constructing the checklist for the performance test.

1. Remember that the examiner must concentrate upon the observation of the student or students to whom the test is being given. The checklist should be designed to require a minimum amount of writing. Make it truly a checklist, not merely a form to receive miscellaneous comments.

2. Make sure that provisions are made for checking the important measurable aspects of effective performance and for reporting on the specific points that are indicative of efficiency with respect to each.

3. Place related items together under appropriate headings, and make provisions for subtotals in the score column to facilitate use of the test for diagnostic purposes. In the section of the checklist to be executed during or immediately following the student's performance, items should occur on the checklist in the same order in which they would normally receive the student's attention as the work is completed.

4. To minimize the problem of weighting, select and group items in the checklist in such a manner as to make each of about the same relative importance as any other in the list. Trivial and insignificant points should be excluded. Avoid complicated procedures for determining the relative point values to be assigned each item in the checklist. Your considered judgment as the teacher, perhaps combined with the judgments of other teachers in your field who thoroughly understand your objectives, will probably be as valid as any other criterion for assigning values to the various items in the checklist.

5. For all items on which students normally vary significantly in efficiency, make provisions for giving appropriate credit for the various discernible degrees of efficiency or quality. Generally, distinctions should be attempted on the basis of not less than three or more than five levels of proficiency. For example, four points might be given for working to within one level of tolerance, three points for another level, two points for yet another level, and one point for the last level, and no credit for an error greater than some specified level. Some elements, however, might involve only two possibilities with respect to the awarding or withholding of credit. In checking upon the selection of the proper tool or instrument, full credit would probably be given if the student selects the one furnished for that purpose and no credit at all if the wrong one is selected.

Quality scales may also be included as a part of the test. These are especially desirable if the test involves several elements whose evaluation must remain dependent upon the judgment of the examiner.

Provide for Time Recording

The checklist should include provisions for recording time consumed and a means of indicating credit or points earned on the basis of time.

Student's Name: _____   Date: _____

Rated by: _____   Score: _____

Workmanship Rating Scale

FB-90° = Forward Bend 90°
45° = 45° Bend
RB-90° = Reverse Bend

	Bends	Points Possible	Given
1. Use the 6' wooden rule, measures within + or − $^{1}/_{8}$"	FB-90° 45° RB-90	2 2 2	
2. Uses pencil, scribes mark entirely around the tube.	FB-90° 45° RB-90°	2 2 2	
3. Uses guide block when cutting with hacksaw.	FB-90° 45° RB-90°	2 2 2	
4. Makes a straight cut without taking hand off tubing cutter, uses rocking motion.	FB-90° 45° RB-90°	2 2 2	
5. Uses reamer properly and removes burrs from ID of tube.	FB-90° 45° RB-90°	2 2 2	
6. Uses file and emery cloth properly, removes burr from OD of tube.	FB-90° 45° RB-90°	2 2 2	
7. Removes metal chips from ID of tube by blowing through tubing.	FB-90° 45° RB-90°	2 2 2	
8. Check for <u>quality</u> of bend, look for kinks, flat spots, or wrinkles in bend. Look for a true 45° and 90° bend.	FB-90° 45° RB-90°	8 8 8	
9. Check center-to-center dimensions of bends. Refer to drawing. Do the bends look like the drawing?	FB-90° 45° RB-90°	8 8 8	

TOTAL POINTS   90

FIGURE 11–5 **Performance Test Rating Sheet**

Prepare Test Administration Directions

Prepare a set of directions for administering the test. Even if the test is to be administered without the aid of assistants, this is a desirable step. First, preparation of the directions will ensure that the details involved in administering the test are thought through. Second, it is of the utmost importance that the same procedure be followed in administering the test to all students. If assistants are to be used or if the test is to be used by several teachers, directions to the examiner are a requirement. This will also serve as a guide for the next administration of the test. Points to be covered in the directions to the test administrator include any special preparation required by the administrator prior to the test administration, and whether the student instructions are to be read aloud by the administrator or silently by the student taking the test. Provision should be made for what to do if time runs out and the task has not been completed. If any assistance may be provided to the student, it should be so indicated in the instructions. The administrator should be informed of the items or equipment that must be collected once the student has completed the task. And most important, directions should indicate all safety precautions to be observed.

Prepare Student Instructions

Prepare a set of directions and instructions for the students. This set of directions should include the following points.

1. State the purpose of the test. It is a common practice to place the student in a work situation by naming a company and the job title being filled. Describe the situation with which the student must deal, the problem to be solved, or the job to be completed.
2. Explain exactly what the student is to do. In some cases you may wish to include in these directions the detailed step-by-step procedure to be followed by the student in performing the test. If, however, the test is designed to measure knowledge of the correct procedure as well as the ability to follow that procedure, include only sufficient details to ensure an understanding of the job requirement.
3. Explain the major factors that will be considered in evaluating the student's performance. The student should know, for instance, the relative importance to be attached to the time element and to such factors as accuracy and following the procedure taught. (See Figures 11–4 and 11–6 for examples of skills to be evaluated and standards to be met by the students in their performance.)

List the Equipment and Supplies Needed

A comprehensive list of all equipment and supplies necessary to complete the examination should be provided on the test form for the students (see Figure 11–7). Include note paper, writing instruments, tools, instruments, software, hardware, ref-

Standard

1. Measure tubing within + or $-\frac{1}{8}''$.
2. Scribe pencil mark entirely around the tube.
3. Use guide block when cutting with hacksaw.
4. Make a straight cut without taking hand off the cutter, by using the "rocking motion" method.
5. Check for burrs on the inside of the tubing.
6. Check for burrs on the outside of the tubing.
7. Blow through tubing to remove chips.
8. Check dimensions with ruler.

FIGURE 11–6 **Standards to Be Met**

erence books, and any other material necessary to complete the performance detailed in the instructions to the student.

Create Answer Templates

Select or construct devices for testing the completed work. Many performance tests are so designed and administered that the student's completed work must be tested or measured and evaluated in order to arrive at the total score on the test. Generally the

All materials and tools will be provided.

1. Coiled rolls of copper tubing ($\frac{1}{4}''$ type M)
2. Lead pencils (No. 2)
3. Wooden rules (6′)
4. Tubing cutters
5. Files (round and flat)
6. Emery cloth
7. Rigid tubing benders
8. Hacksaw
9. Guide block

FIGURE 11–7 **Example of Materials Needed**

ordinary measuring devices used in the occupation or discipline will serve adequately to obtain measures of accuracy.

Try out the Test

Try the test, and subject it to the criticism of others. Rarely does one individual construct a performance test that is free of flaws the first time it is administered. If you are in a position to subject your performance tests to the criticisms of other teachers in your field, you can obtain many helpful suggestions. Make an analysis of the results obtained the first few times each test is administered. Experience in administering a test will enable you to make intelligent adjustments in such items as time limitations, tolerances, and the specific aspects of the students' performance that should be noted and checked.

To illustrate the procedures presented in this chapter, a performance test that was constructed using all points covered above is included in Appendix A.

ADMINISTERING MANIPULATIVE PERFORMANCE TESTS

Because manipulative performance tests as discussed in this chapter are so different from paper-and-pencil tests, their administration is covered in the following section. Chapter 12 discusses the administration and scoring of other types of tests.

Regardless of how well constructed a performance test may be, the reliability and validity of results obtained with it remain dependent upon the skill of the examiner who administers the test. The mere fact that a detailed checklist has been constructed and specific directions prepared for both the student and examiner will not ensure satisfactory test results. The examiner must be able to remember, keep in mind, and look for evidence of application of specific details.

In addition to skill in observing the details of performance and in recording the results of the observation, there are other important requirements to be met in administering a performance test. Following are some specific suggestions.

1. If possible, set up a sufficient number of identical stations and make use of assistants so that the performance test can be administered to the entire group to be tested in one class period. The complexity of the operations and the nature of the equipment required will determine the number of students who can be tested at one time by one instructor. Generally not more than five or six students can be checked at a time. In a one-hour period an instructor can hardly administer a twelve-minute performance test to more than twenty-four students. Figure 11–8 provides an example of a test administration layout.

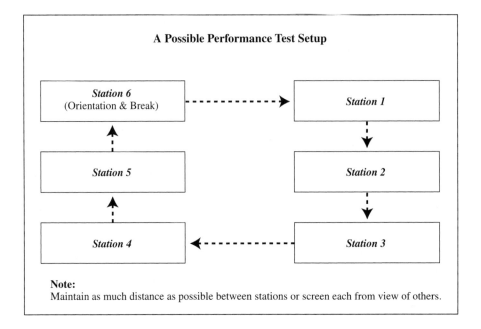

FIGURE 11–8   **Performance Test Setup**

2. Since the matter of ensuring sufficient difficulty to obtain a significant range of test scores is not generally a problem in constructing performance tests, it is important that tools, materials, and equipment selected for the test be of good quality, in excellent condition, and free of faults that would handicap students. All machines, equipment, and instruments should be carefully checked to make sure that they are in proper condition.

3. Make sure that conditions will be the same for each student. Each should have materials of the same quality and working characteristics and access to tools and equipment of the same kind and condition. There should be nothing at any test station that would penalize the particular student assigned to that station.

4. Plan profitable activities to occupy the time of students who will be waiting their turns to take the test. These activities should be such that students waiting to take the test will not have an opportunity to do additional studying that may be prompted by the directions to the test. Also plan work to be performed by students who will have completed the test early.

5. Carefully read and explain the directions to the entire group. If possible, provide each student with a copy of the directions. The purposes of the test will determine whether or not the checklist will be made available to the students.

6. Do not permit students who have already completed the test to discuss the test with students who are taking or waiting to take the test.

7. Study the checklist prior to the administration of the test. Know exactly what to observe and what to record as the student takes the test.

8. If the time element is a factor in the student's score, record the time accurately. Record the exact time as the student begins the test, and again when the test is finished. The difference in minutes can be computed later.

9. Check all students against the same predetermined standards. As a check against your ability to do this, try filling out a second checklist for each of a few students, without reference to the original checklist, and then compare the results.

10. If several students are to take the test at one time, arrange the stations to minimize interference. All stations to be supervised by one instructor should be clearly visible from a central point.

11. Evaluate all completed work at one time and by the same predetermined standards.

12. Rather than permit a student to commit an error that would prevent going on with the test or would prove unsafe, stop the student and provide the instructions necessary to eliminate the difficulty, then allow the student to continue. Give no credit, however, for the part of the performance that required your assistance.

13. After the test has been administered and scored, discuss with the class outstanding strengths and weaknesses noted. Give the students an opportunity to ask questions and clear up any misunderstandings.

All elements of a performance test as described in this section and illustrated in the figures can be found in Appendix A, where they are arranged in a more coherent, user-friendly order.

SUMMARY

If the development of manipulative skill is an objective for a course, then some means must be devised for measuring and evaluating the extent to which skill has been developed. The performance test is one means of measuring this outcome. It is prepared specifically to measure the students' skill in the performance of selected operations under controlled conditions.

The performance test should be constructed and administered in such a manner as to measure speed, quality of work, and the appropriateness of the procedures followed.

The following are the major steps involved in the construction of a performance test:

1. Select operations to be incorporated in the performance test.

2. Make a preliminary analysis of each operation selected.

3. Select or design a job that includes the operations selected.

4. Prepare a drawing and/or specifications for a job.
5. List all specific points feasible for testing purposes.
6. Select the specific points to be incorporated in the test.
7. Construct a checklist that includes one section to be executed as the student performs, and another to record the results of a careful analysis of the student's completed work.
8. Prepare a set of directions to be followed by the students.
9. Prepare a set of directions for administering the test.
10. Select or construct devices for testing the student's completed work.
11. Try out the test, and subject it to the criticism of others.

If well prepared and carefully administered, the performance test can be used to obtain a highly objective, reliable, and valid measure of the student's ability to perform certain selected operations. It provides a detailed analysis of the student's performance, as application is made of things taught in the classroom. On the other hand, it has definite limitations and disadvantages. Remember that the mere fact that a given performance test requires actual performance on the part of the student does not necessarily make it a good test. Results are dependent to a great extent upon the manner in which the test is constructed and, especially, upon the training, experience, and skill of the instructor who administers it.

DISCUSSION QUESTIONS

1. To what extent are the reliability and validity of results obtained with performance tests dependent upon the skill of the person who administers the tests?

2. What factors should be taken into consideration in selecting operations to be incorporated in a performance test? What changes would you suggest in the list of criteria included in this chapter?

3. Describe performance-test situations in which the procedure followed by the student should be given more weight than the quality of the finished job.

4. Aside from the validity of the measurement obtained, what advantages does the performance test have over written tests for the purpose of measuring the student's ability to do skilled manipulative work?

5. Why is it considered unwise to use the performance test as the only means of measuring and evaluating manipulative skills? What other means should be used along with performance tests?

6. How would you check the reliability of a performance test? The validity?

7. How would you obtain group judgments as a basis for weighting various phases of a performance test?

8. What are major difficulties involved in administering performance tests?

EXERCISES

1. Prepare a short performance test to measure proficiency in the performance of one or two simple operations selected from your subject area. Have at least five different persons whom you consider competent to administer the test observe and score a student's performance and the completed job. Compare the results obtained by the five persons. What are the implications of the results?

2. Select from the subject matter of your own area of interest several tasks that require students to perform manipulative skills. State in measurable terms a student performance objective for each of those tasks. List in chronological order the steps necessary to complete each task from start to finish. In a separate paragraph, describe the knowledge and attitudes a person would have to possess in order to complete the task successfully.

3. Construct a performance examination to assess several of the psychomotor performance objectives for your course or program. For example, this examination might be to assess a student's performance on administering CPR, typing a manuscript, adjusting brakes, taking a dental impression, or shooting baskets. Include a checklist for use in observing the examination and all necessary directions to students and observers. The checklist should have a rating scale that indicates the degree to which the specific performance is attained.

RESOURCES

A Reference List and Selected Bibliography

Hill, P., Harvey, J., & Praskac, A. (1994). Pandora's box: Accountability and performance standards in vocational education. Berkeley, CA: National Center for Research in Vocational Education, University of California at Berkeley.

Mitchell, R. (1992). *Testing for learning: How new approaches to evaluation can improve American schools.* New York: Macmillan; Free Press.

► 12

Test Construction, Administration, and Scoring

Now that you have learned the rules for specific kinds of items used in tests, it is time to build your test, administer and score it, and check to see if it worked as planned. All items in all tests (and all assignments and projects) given in class should be valid, reliable, objective, and practical. They *must* relate to and measure behavior that is specified in the objectives. For tests, the types of items used should be chosen with an understanding of student ability, the nature of the subject matter, the course objectives, and the time available. Some general rules for test construction follow.

Previous chapters of this book have made the point that if a test is to be valid, reliable, and objective, and if it is to be comprehensive, discriminating, and easily administered and scored, a definite, systematic procedure must be followed in its construction. This means more than paging through a textbook and picking out sentences or paragraphs from which to construct the test items.

As previously stated, the construction of a test is basically a twofold process: first determining what should be measured and then devising measuring instruments (items) that will best do the job. This step-by-step procedure is applicable both in constructing short unit tests and in devising comprehensive examinations. An elaboration of this process is given below. Following this outline, a series of specific points is presented to serve as suggestions and reminders as the actual test construction is carried out.

STEPS TO FOLLOW IN BUILDING A TEST

List the Major Course Objectives for Which an Appraisal Is Desired

One technique for doing this is to put the objectives in question form. If the objectives are in the cognitive domain, a written examination will be necessary. Some cognitive ability or knowledge can be surmised from actions on a performance test, but construction of the checklist to determine this is difficult and may make observation of more than one student at a time impossible. A good guideline to follow is "If the objective is in the cognitive domain, use a written test."

Examine the Course Content for Additional Objectives

This is a checking step to make sure that all objectives are listed. Consult the course objectives, the course of study, the textbook, and other sources. If a content analysis (recall Figure 1–1) of the basic skills and knowledge used in the occupation or the subject is available, it will prove helpful as a reminder of what the objectives should have been if they were not clearly articulated.

Analyze and Define Each Objective in Terms of Expected Student Outcome or Behavior

This is an inventory step where the elements that are a part of each objective are listed. Define each element in terms of student behavior, that is, the learning domain and the level of learning within that domain (see Chapter 2). List items of subject matter related to each element. This step will take time and will involve considerable detail, but once accomplished it will contain information useful time and again as the course is taught and retaught.

Establish a Table of Specifications

This blueprint for construction of individual test items will serve as a guide by helping to indicate the emphasis that should be given to each objective in terms of numbers of items. Develop an outline of the test that you are planning to construct. Do this in the same fashion as you would a lesson plan in order to make sure that all objectives are tested. Figure 12–1 contains an example of a partial table of specifications for a test. The first column of the table lists the course objectives that are to be represented on the test. The course calls for performance at all the levels of learning, so they are all included in the table of specifications. The column for each level of learning shows the number of test items for that level. The last two columns contain the total number of items for each objective and percentage of the total items for

Course	Levels of Learning			Total	% of Total
Objective	General	Working	Qualified	Number	Items
1	2	2	1	5	10
2	2	1	1	4	8
3	2	3	2	7	14
4	2	2	1	5	10
5	2	2	2	6	12
6	3	1	0	4	8
7	2	2	1	5	10
8	2	3	1	6	12
9	2	2	0	4	8
10	2	1	1	4	8
Total	21	19	10	50	
% of Total Items	42	38	29		100%

FIGURE 12–1   **Partial Table of Test Specifications**

each objective on the test. Because some objectives may be more complex or may be deemed more important than others, the number of test items will vary.

Omitting this step in test construction will surely save time, but it is not recommended because it is the only way to insure: (1) that all pertinent objectives are assessed, and (2) that balance will be achieved among the several levels of learning being assessed. A complete table of test specifications is an important step in developing valid tests.

Construct One or More Test Items for Each Objective Listed

Determine which type(s) of test item will best measure the extent to which each specific objective has been attained. The number of items for any one objective will depend upon the nature of the objective. This step will take considerable time and is one that should be on going as the course is taught. In other words, items should be developed as material is taught and learned, not the night before the examination is to be given.

An important point to remember is that the objective to be measured comes first; *then* the type of test item that will best do the job is determined. This may sound obvious, but time after time teachers start out to make twenty-five true-false items, then fifteen multiple-choice, then twenty completion, and so on. That is, they begin by selecting a type of test item and then try to find some subject matter to fit, which is a common but illogical approach to test construction.

Carrying out this step may result in several types of test items. If there are only a few items of certain types, these can be revised and adapted to other types of items that are to be used. A general rule is to include no more than three or four types of items in a single test. There are exceptions to this rule, however, and additional types might be justified by the test maker.

Assemble the Items for the Test

After grouping the items by types, arrange them so that related items are together. For example, suppose that in a given test you have four multiple-choice items related to one particular subject. These should be placed together rather than scattered throughout the multiple-choice section. This saves student time as the test is taken, and helps students keep in the same frame of mind.

Sometimes it is tempting to try to arrange the items according to difficulty, but item difficulty is a relative factor. Any item will be difficult if the student has not studied the material or if the teacher forgot to mention or has not taught the point well. At best, the difficulty level of individual items in an informal teacher-made test can be determined only after thorough use and reuse of the test. From a practical standpoint, then, little will be gained at the start by trying to arrange the items in the order of difficulty.

Write Clear and Concise Directions for Each Type of Question

The directions should tell the students what they are to do, how they are to do it, and where they are to place the responses. For at least the first few tests students take from a teacher, the directions should also contain an example taken from the subject matter being tested. (Sample directions for the several types of test items were included in the chapters for each type of item.) Tell the students the purpose of the test and the type of questions they will encounter. If you do not want them to write on the test itself, tell them so here. Inform them that specific instructions will be provided for each type of question.

Study Every Aspect of the Assembled Test

After the test is assembled and the directions are written, it is a good practice to lay it aside for several days, then pick it up again and review each part critically. Try to consider each item from the point of view of the students who will take the test. See if you can determine those items that may be ambiguous. Check on the grammar. Ask yourself questions such as the following:

1. Does each item really measure the students' attainment of the objective?
2. If not, how could it be revised to do so?
3. Is each set of directions clear? Do the directions apply to every item in the group, or do some items require specific directions?
4. Is there plenty of space to write the response?

Construct the Answer Key

In constructing the answer key, keep in mind the procedure to be followed in scoring the test. This process may lead to the decision to revise certain items to make them easier to score.

Have Other Teachers Critique and, if Possible, Actually Take the Test

This step, carried out conscientiously, will provide valuable suggestions for improving the validity of the test. If there is not time to do this, take the test yourself.

Make Any Necessary Revisions

Change any items or procedures that cause confusion, take too much time, or otherwise cause the test to be less effective.

After the Test Has Been Administered, Analyze and Improve It

Conduct an item analysis (see "Analyzing and Interpreting Test Results" later in this chapter). Correct any weaknesses that are revealed through item analysis and observation of the students as they take the test. Tests and test items should be analyzed, revised, and improved each time they are used.

These steps have been presented briefly and almost in outline form after having been presented in somewhat different form in earlier chapters on specific item types. The importance of following a logical, step-by-step procedure in test construction cannot be understated.

CARD-FILE TEST BUILDING

A useful technique for building better tests is to develop a card file of effective test items. If you can't find any cards, or if you like working with your computer better, this process works equally well using any wordprocessing program or computerized test-construction software. In building a card file of test items the teacher assumes that there are certain objectives that will be stable and therefore can be listed before any specific test is actually constructed. This is usually a valid assumption. In the same fashion, many desirable attitudes, habits, and appreciations can be identified. After all these have been listed, it is possible to prepare a variety of test items that might be used in measuring each point. Each item is placed on a single card and filed under an appropriate heading (see Figure 12–2). The correct answer should be indicated on the test item card in some fashion, such as using an asterisk or drawing a circle around the letter. When it comes time to prepare a specific test, the objectives to be measured are listed. Then the card file is consulted to find all the possible items that can be used to measure the objectives. If the card file is complete, this process will result in many more items than are needed or wanted. It is then necessary simply to select the best ones. Some slight revisions might be needed, or some additional items might have to be constructed to measure an objective peculiar to a certain group. Even so, it is easy to see how much time can be saved by means of a complete and well-prepared file of items.

The process of building a file of items is simple, but carrying it out takes time and effort. It may take a year or two to build up a file that is relatively complete and contains valid and reliable items, but in the long run it saves a great deal of time. Improvements will always be called for, but once the system is well organized, a test can easily be assembled for any purpose and in a much shorter time than would otherwise be possible.

Use one card for each item when building the file. Items such as matching or

---

The correct answer should be indicated on the test item card in some fashion, such as using an asterisk or drawing a circle around the letter.

Test anxiety:

A. is always detrimental to test performance.

B. generally causes an examinee to work harder.

C. is more of a problem for some examinees than others.*

D. should be eliminated on good objective tests.

FIGURE 12–2   **Sample Test Item Card**

cluster true-false will also be put on one card, although there may be several points to the item. The best size of card is perhaps 5x8 inches, although this is relative to the teacher's needs. A 3x5- or 4x6-inch card could be used for many of the items, but the larger size will make for uniformity and will provide plenty of space for most of the longer items, and there will still be room to jot down figures and notes about the effectiveness of the items.

Figure 12–3 indicates the make-up of a typical card file of test items. The file headings shown are illustrative of those from several different subject areas. Yours will all be in one subject, or several closely related subjects or courses. The manner in which the items are grouped will be dependent upon the purposes of the test maker. Grouping the items under subject-matter headings would seem to be more logical and useful than to group them by types of items. A simple process—imposing a standard color scheme—will make the types of items readily identifiable. This is accomplished by sorting out all the cards with the same type of item, holding them firmly together, and marking the tops of all with a large felt-tip marker. Each item is then filed under the appropriate heading. Suppose the multiple-choice color is red. It would be easy to select the multiple-choice items under a given subject merely by picking out the red-topped cards. This same process could be followed for any type of item.

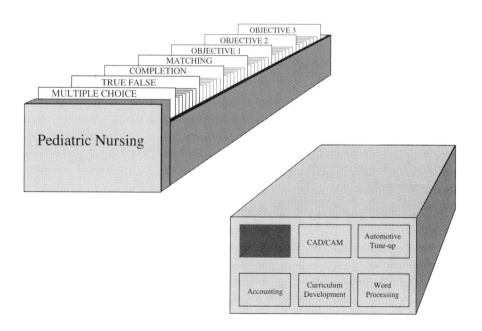

FIGURE 12–3 **Card File Illustration**

ONE LAST SET OF RULES

It should now be evident that there are many specific points to keep in mind when constructing an examination. Some of these points have been covered already in the chapters on specific item types, and others are grouped here to facilitate the planning and construction of a test.

The following suggestions are not listed in the order of their importance, and you may note some repetition of points previously discussed in the chapters on specific types of items. The answers to some of the common questions asked by beginning test makers are found here. A working knowledge of the following suggestions will serve as an effective checklist that will be helpful in constructing tests.

It is not possible to measure all instructional outcomes with one type of test. Be wary of trying to measure the development of manipulative skills with a written test. A good performance test is much more effective for such purposes. It is also not advisable to try to measure cognitive gain by using performance tests. Careful and systematic observation of students in nontest situations will often provide a measure of the acquisition of certain traits that written tests can seldom, if ever, provide (see Chapter 13). Written tests do not measure everything that teachers need to know about students or student progress. They must be used wisely, and their results must be interpreted with a full knowledge of the limitations that exist.

Make tests comprehensive, but exclude insignificant and trivial items. This means sampling the whole range of instruction in a unit. When there is an urge to put an item in a test simply because it will add one more point to the total score or give a nice even number of items, stop and reconsider. Typical teacher-made tests contain too many items that have no real significance—items that are trivial and unimportant. The best they do is to provide a smoke screen through which it is difficult to ascertain real gain or subject mastery. If the steps suggested in the previous section are followed, there should be little need to question the comprehensiveness of the completed test.

Write the items so they require the student actually to apply concepts or materials learned, rather than merely to recall or recognize facts. This point has been made several times already and it is one of the most important to keep in mind. If an entire test consisted of questions that simply required students to recall or recognize, the results might appear to indicate excellent mastery of the subject, while in fact their understanding would only be low-level, superficial, and inadequate.

Make certain that the type of test item used for measuring each objective is the one that will best measure that objective. Once again, this means that the objective is developed first and the test item second. No single type of test item is superior for all kinds of measurement; certain types have advantages over others, but these are specific advantages in specific situations. Strive to make each test item the best one for that particular job.

Avoid trick, or "catch," questions. Some teachers like to include puzzling items in which hidden meanings or subtle clues provide the correct responses. These items

PEANUTS By Charles M. Schulz

PEANUTS reprinted by permission of UFS, Inc.

are neither fair to the students, nor are they valid measures of subject mastery. All that such items indicate is the ability of certain students to see through the smoke screen set up by the teacher.

This does not mean that all items must be easy to answer. It does mean that if the students know the point in question they should be able to answer the item immediately without having to "psych out" the teacher. Remember that classroom tests are trying to measure subject mastery, not intelligence. The purpose is to find out how much the students have learned, not how easily they can be tripped up.

Include a large number of items in the test. This tends to increase the reliability. Of course, one should not include more items just for the sake of adding points. The exact number of items to use in any given test will depend upon the purpose of the test and the types of items selected. A few carefully prepared multiple-choice items may be much more valid and reliable than a large number of true-false questions prepared in a hurry. With this qualification in mind, the suggestion still holds—include a large number of items. Remember, each test must be comprehensive enough to be valid. Use as many items as necessary to cover the subject or the objectives and no more. It is not a sin or an inconvenience to have odd numbers of items on a test. Items at all levels of difficulty should be used, but the first one or two items on the completed test should be easy items to get everyone off to a good, successful start.

Do not take statements directly from books to use as test items. This is a common practice in many teacher-made tests. Sometimes an entire test will be constructed by paging through a book and selecting isolated sentences or paragraphs that seem appropriate. Perhaps the statements are to be used in a true-false test and are changed slightly to make them false. Very often one or two significant words will be replaced by a dash, and the statement then becomes a completion-type item. Such a practice should be scrupulously avoided.

The weakness of such items lies in the fact that students can provide the correct response without knowing what the response really means. This same point was illustrated in discussing the necessity of devising items that call for application rather than mere memorization. When a student receives a high score on a test that is constructed in such a fashion, it may only mean that the student has a good short-term memory and no ability to apply the material.

Check to make sure that no item can be answered simply by referring to other items. It is easy for this to happen unless a careful check is made. Such relationships are not always obvious, especially when numerous items intervene, but the students with good memories will find such hints and weakness in tests that have not been checked carefully.

Make each item independent of the others. Do not have the correct answer to one item dependent upon the answer to another. The items may well be related to each other, but a right or wrong answer to one should not automatically result in a similar answer to the other. Create items so that a student who marked the wrong answer to item 1 does not automatically get the wrong answer for item 2. When such questions are used, a slight mistake is doubled. The student may know the correct procedure or process, but a wrong answer to the first part leads to a wrong answer to the second part.

Do not include items to which the answer is obvious to someone who does not know the subject matter. This highlights a common fault in test making: Many tests include items that could be answered easily by intelligent people even though they might know nothing at all about the subject matter.

Be careful of specific determiners. Such words as *all, never, always, none, alone, may,* and *should* act as specific determiners in true-false items. Some students will note such qualifying words immediately and will mark their responses accordingly. Unless the test maker corrects such deficiencies in true-false items, the alert student will be able to get a high score without knowing much about the subject matter involved. This fault is not confined to true-false questions. Matching items often contain answers that are just as obvious.

Word the items in the simplest manner possible. Confine the terms used to the vocabulary level of the students. While this suggestion is applicable to any test item, particular attention should be paid to the wording of items containing technical information. The wording of items and the selection of terms and expressions are a relative matter, requiring judgment on the part of the test maker. The best general rule is to word each item as simply as possible.

State questions clearly and eliminate ambiguous items. Sometimes an entire item is poorly constructed and needs to be completely revised. Very often the clarity can be improved by changing a word or phrase. For the beginning test maker, the important consideration is to keep in mind the students who will be responding to the items. At best, it is a difficult process to construct a series of statements that will be interpreted with some degree of uniformity by a group of people.

Keep the method of recording responses as simple as possible. The manner of answering test items can be more difficult for the student than recalling or recognizing the information needed to make the response. Involved methods of indicating responses tend to measure general intelligence rather than subject mastery. For example, the controlled-completion type of item is usually confusing to students when they see it for the first time so careful explanation should be given in the directions. If such explanations are not provided, test items are apt to be answered in an odd variety of ways.

Leave sufficient space for all responses without crowding. Having to crowd several words in a small space is hard on the student and also makes the job of correcting more difficult. The easiest way to avoid this fault is to make sure that, before the test is given, a complete key is made to bring such faults to light.

When answering directly on the test form, arrange blanks for responses along one side of the page. This facilitates scoring. The left side of the page is used in most instances since the blanks will be next to the item number and there will be less chance for errors on the part of the student. If the test maker feels that a certain type of item arranged in this manner will be confusing to the students, then a different arrangement should be employed. If a separate answer sheet is used, this suggestion need not be considered.

Use a separate answer sheet whenever possible. An answer sheet that is separate from the test contains numbered blanks for the students to fill in. There are numerous variations. The two major advantages of answer sheets are: (1) They make for easier and more rapid scoring and (2) the tests themselves can be used again. A separate answer sheet allows correction of the test without turning hundreds of pages and trying to match items with a key. Many teachers who do not use separate answer sheets find out two-thirds of the way through correcting an examination that on the third paper they "corrected" their key from a student's paper! Needless to say, they have to start over.

Arrange the items so that responses will not form a particular pattern. This means that there should not be five true items, followed by five false items, followed by five true items, and so on. Likewise, in multiple-choice items it is not desirable to have the first two items answered by the fifth choice, the next two by the fourth choice, and so on. Answers to questions should form a random pattern. Many people have favorite letters that are unconsciously used as the correct answer when making up test items. (Have you ever heard the phrase, When in doubt, mark "C"?) Examine your items to detect this tendency and rearrange as necessary. Most computer-based test programs will automatically randomize answer patterns.

Arrange the items so that students will not have to refer to more than one page in answering a given item. Adherence to this suggestion will save students time and avoid confusion. It is much better to *not* use three or four lines of a sheet of paper than to have the students turning pages over and back while trying to determine what goes where. Multiple-choice answer possibilities should be arranged vertically rather than run all altogether horizontally. This too will require a bit more paper to reproduce the test, but it will be much easier to read and to take. Most of the time a slight revision of the items will result in satisfactory page placement with no loss of space. If you are lucky enough to have assistance, the person who will prepare the test should pay careful attention to this suggestion. Remember, the purpose of testing is to determine students' mastery of the subject, not their ability to wade through a maze of words. Computer test-construction programs automatically eliminate this problem.

Number the responses consecutively from the beginning to the end of the test. When each part of the test is numbered separately, it is more difficult to identify a particular item, especially when the test is being analyzed with the students for the purpose of improvement. The usual practice is to have only one set of consecutive numbers, 1 through X.

The practice of <u>underlining</u> crucial words, if not done too frequently and indiscriminately, tends to increase the objectivity of test items. By underlining certain words, an otherwise ambiguous statement may become clear to the students. Students do not have to spend time thinking about the form of the item and are able to concentrate on the content.

Avoid weighting the items. Each single response should be numbered and should count one point. Almost invariably the beginning test maker will want to argue about this suggestion by saying that some points of subject matter are more important than others and therefore should receive more credit when answered correctly in a test. It *is* true that certain objectives may be relatively more important than others, but the research that has been conducted on this subject indicates that little, if anything, is gained by taking the time to assign different weights to different types of items. In either case, the rank order of the student responses will be almost exactly the same. This means that it is not worth the effort for the typical classroom teacher to try to assign weights to test items. If a certain objective is especially important, require the student to respond to several situations in which it is tested. In other words, give one point for each item, but devise several items that bear on the particular objective.

If the test is to be corrected for guessing, indicate this clearly in the directions. When a correction formula is used, the students should be instructed not to guess and to omit those items they are unable to answer. Correction formulas can be applied to all types of test items but are usually associated with two-response items. The question of whether or not to correct for guessing is difficult to answer. Research studies of this question have indicated that the validity of *standardized* tests tend to be raised slightly when a correction for guessing is carried out, but there isn't much evidence to indicate that criterion-referenced classroom tests are significantly improved by correcting for guessing. From a purely statistical standpoint, the procedure might be justified, but in terms of the meaning of a single test score, it is a practice of doubtful value. There is usually little to be gained in using correction formulas with teacher-made informal tests, especially when the time it takes to do so is considered.

For some purposes (such as when using standardized tests) a corrected score may well be justified, but at the same time it may be a poor indication of actual attainment. If the "right minus wrong" formula is used, it is possible for the student to mark one-half the items right and still obtain a score of zero. It is likewise possible for one student to have more correct responses than another, yet receive a lower total score. To be sure, the student may have guessed more items, but he or she also knew more items. In addition, the guesses may have been made on the basis of partial knowledge of the subject being tested. The question is whether the corrected or uncorrected score is the best indication of achievement.

Very few students will conscientiously omit items they do not know. For this reason the total score will tend to be lower than actual attainment would warrant. Uncorrected scores would allow for guessing and thus make the total scores higher than they should be. Of the two faults it would seem best to err in the students' favor. The best solution is to avoid using the common true-false items and let the laws of chance operate with the others.

Make sure the directions are clear and complete. Each test should contain a set of general instructions or directions that tell the students the number and type of items, the number of pages making up the test, and the amount of time available for taking the test. The general directions should also tell the students how and where to place their responses. Students should be told to inspect the test before beginning and what to do when finished. As the students learn the testing procedures in a given class, the general directions can become less specific, or in some cases can be eliminated altogether.

Directions should be provided for each type of item on the test. It is often a good idea to include an example in the item-specific directions to show the students what is wanted. A large number of incorrect responses can be traced directly either to the students' failure to understand the directions or to failure to read them carefully. In selecting examples to show the students, take them from the subject matter of the test and make them meaningful. Use the examples to teach certain points. Sample directions for the various types of test items are found in the chapters on each item.

Prepare a proper heading for the test. The heading should provide an identification of the test, space for the student's name and total score, plus any other information that will be useful. A general rule is to make the heading as simple as possible while providing the needed data. Most computer test-construction programs provide sample headings that are easily modified for any test.

ADMINISTERING THE TEST

The validity and reliability of any test are affected to some extent by the conditions under which it is given. The test area should be well lighted, well ventilated, and quiet. All materials necessary for taking the test should be provided, and all materials should be the same or of equivalent quality. All students should have the opportunity of taking the same test under the best possible conditions. If consideration needs to be made for students with special needs, it should be thought of well in advance and carried out.

The following rules for test administration are general and are recommended specifically for written tests, although they will often apply to performance tests.

Attitude

The teacher should maintain a cheerful, relaxed demeanor and encourage the students to view the test as a challenge rather than as a trial by fire. If this attitude prevails, students will usually do better and the results will be more valid.

Distractions

All training aids, chalkboard drawings, models, notes, and other distractions in the test room should be covered or removed. Students should be instructed to put notes and books away, unless the test is an open-book examination wherein part of the examination will test the students' ability to use reference materials.

Cheating

Take precautions to prevent cheating. Position students so that it is difficult to whisper or to see another student's paper. Do not allow materials other than those necessary to take the test to be on top of the desks or work stations. Distribute all test materials according to a seating plan. In some situations, it is advisable to number test booklets and hand one to each student individually. Make sure that students turn in the booklet that they were issued. The best way to reduce cheating is to reduce the opportunity for it to occur—to maintain control of the classroom at all times.

Instructions

Provide complete and clear oral instructions for taking the test. It is a good idea to read aloud any written instructions in order to ensure that all students receive the correct instructions and have the opportunity to ask questions on points they do not understand. This is infinitely better than having a number of students raise their hands and ask questions during the exam time. Often, when students are in a hurry while taking the test, they will only give superficial attention to the written instructions.

Supervision

The teacher should maintain quiet supervision of all students taking the test. It is best to find a position so that all students can be seen, and take action or move around only as the need arises. Patrolling the room gives the impression that you are suspicious or distrustful, and distracts the students from the task at hand. If students are allowed to leave the room after they complete the test, advise them in the oral instructions not to talk to you as they leave or to make other distractions while other students are still taking the test.

SCORING THE TEST

Many schools have equipment and supplies for the machine scoring of tests. For the most part, though, teachers have to score (or correct) tests by hand. Thus the teacher's life is made easier if separate answer sheets are developed and used for each test.

A scoring stencil can be easily made for correcting multiple-choice, true-false, and matching items. Often, an answer sheet that has holes punched to indicate the correct answer will suffice. When the stencil is placed over the answer sheets, incorrectly marked answers do not show, but the marked correct answer shows through the hole. A simple count (after scoring) of the unmarked choices that occur at the holes is the number of answers missed by the student.

Completion, or short answer, items are usually scored by using a strip of paper that has the correct answer on it. This strip is spaced according to the blank lines on the answer sheet and is laid alongside those lines for a quick comparison of the students' answers with the correct answers.

Before scoring any tests, it is a good practice to scan all answer sheets to see if more than one answer has been marked per item. Count all items wrong that have more than one answer marked. Use colored pencil or felt markers for correcting examinations. After using the stencil or strip sheet for correcting, total all items with two or more answers and those with incorrect answers or those left unanswered. Subtract this total from the total number of test items. The remainder is the student's score, which should be written at the top of the answer sheet.

ANALYZING AND INTERPRETING TEST RESULTS

Now that the tests have been scored, you are left with a pile of papers that have raw scores, or the number correct out of the total number of items on the test. Raw test scores in themselves are meaningless: They must be analyzed, compared, and reviewed in order to be useful. Elementary statistical principles are used to accomplish these purposes. It is necessary to review some of the terminology here.

The *raw score* is simply the number of correct responses on a test. Raw scores are useful when comparing results of a single test, but are meaningless as a basis for comparing results of more than one test because each different test will have a different raw score total. For example, 50 correct responses on a 60-item test is not comparable to 50 correct responses on a 100 item test.

The *range* is the difference between the highest and the lowest scores on a test. For example, if the lowest scoring student on a 100-point test gets 70 correct, and the highest gets 96 correct, the range is 96 – 70 plus 1, or 27. The 1 is added to the difference because the score point actually extends one-half point below the number and one-half point above the number—from 69.5 to 96.5. Thus, 96.5 – 69.5 equals 27. The range is an important part of any test analysis, because extreme ranges might indicate learning or teaching difficulties or misunderstandings.

Three measures of central tendency are important in test analysis. The *mean* is the average score on a test and is determined by adding all scores and dividing the sum by the number of persons who took the test. The mean score of a test is useful for comparing level of student mastery of the subject and for determining differences in teaching and learning. The *median* is the score at the midpoint between the highest and lowest scores on a test. The *mode* is the score that was achieved most often. (See Figure 12–4, discussed below.)

The *interval* is the point, or points, at which various scores are recorded when making a distribution of test scores. The *deviation* is the numerical distance or difference between intervals on a distribution. The *frequency* is the number of times a particular score is recorded on a distribution.

The *percentage score* is the percentage of correct responses on a test. It is determined by dividing the total number of test items into the raw scores. Percentage scores are more useful than raw scores when comparing results of several tests. A *percentile score* is a method of ranking student performance. Percentile scores compare the success of one student to the success of others. For example, a percentile score of 82 indicates that the person who achieved this score did better than 82 percent of the students who took the test. Percentile scores are generally not valid for comparison purposes where small numbers of students are involved, such as in classroom tests. They are, however, used in almost all standardized tests, and teachers should have a general understanding of what they mean.

The first step in analyzing test results is to make a distribution of the scores. This is accomplished by arranging the scores from the highest to the lowest and then making a tally of each person achieving each score. For instance, a distribution could be plotted for a 100-item test as in Figure 12–4. In this example, *raw score intervals* are expressed by the numbers below the line, and students who achieved various raw scores are identified by the x's. The relevant statistics from the information in Figure 12–4 are:

range   =   the highest score − lowest score + 1,
            or $90 - 70 = 20 + 1 = 21$
mean   =   the sum of all the scores divided by the number of students who
            took the test, or $1906 / 24 = 79.42$
median =   the midpoint between the highest and lowest score, or 80

```
                            X
                X           X   X   X           X
            X   X   X   X   X   X           X
    X   X   X   X   X   X   X   X   X   X   X
    ─────────────────────────────────────────────
    70  72  74  76  78  80  82  84  86  88  90
```

FIGURE 12–4   **Distribution of a 100-Item Test**

The distribution of test scores provides a visual means of comparing low, average, and high scores. Large groups of scores at the low end of a test distribution might indicate a test that was too difficult, or one that tested material not covered or not covered well. Large groups at the high end of the distribution might indicate that the test was too easy or that the teacher did an exceptional job of teaching the material and the students an exceptional job of learning it.

The next step in test analysis is to analyze each item. This is done to determine how difficult each item is and how well it discriminates between good and poor students. Item analysis is a relatively simple process. First, arrange the test papers or answer sheets by rank order of scores, lowest to highest. Select the papers with the ten highest scores and those with the ten lowest scores, or the top and bottom 25 percent if you have very large groups. If there are fewer than twenty cases, divide the papers in half. It helps to prepare analysis sheets such as the ones shown in Figures 12–5 and 12–6.

The sheet reproduced in Figure 12–5 is used to analyze the results of a test item by item. Once the papers have been divided into the high and low groups, each of the students' wrong responses to individual items is recorded on the sheet. For example, item 1 is a multiple-choice item, and the answer is "D." In the space on the top half of the diagonal line in each cell, the numbers of students in the high group who marked the item wrong and used answer choices "A," "B," "C," and "E" are tallied. Then the numbers of students in the low group who got the item wrong are also indicated along with their answer choices on the bottom side of the diagonal. This will show how the students marked the answers, not just that they got it wrong. The test maker is then able to see at a glance which of the answer choices are good distractors and which are just giveaways. It also provides a quick picture of which items discriminate and the direction they discriminate in. A complete form that can be duplicated may be found in Appendix B.

ITEM #	T A	F B	C	D	E	NUMBER WRONG	NUMBER RIGHT

FIGURE 12–5 **Item Analysis Sheet**

ITEM	NUMBER CORRECT HIGH	LOW	H+L	H+L/N	DIFFICULTY	ANALYSIS
1.						
2.						
3.						
4.						
5.	8	3	11	11/20	.55	OK
6.						
7.						
8.						
9.						
10.						

FIGURE 12–6　**Item or Test Analysis Calculation Sheet**

After the individual response patterns to items have been discerned, it is an easy task to transfer the numbers to another analysis sheet, such as that shown in Figure 12–6. In the "High" column, record the number of times each item was answered *correctly* by the high scoring group. Record in the "Low" column the number of times each item was answered *correctly* by the low scoring group. Item by item, add the total number of correct responses and enter that figure in the "High + Low" column. Then, for each item, divide the latter figure by the total number of individuals in both the high and low group. If you used the top 10 and the bottom 10, the number (N) would be 20. For example, assume that on item 5, eight students in the high group and three students in the low group got it correct; 8 plus 3 is 11, divided by 20 equals .55. The decimal achieved should always be between 0 and 1.0. A 1.0 would mean that all students got the item correct, a 0.0 would mean that no one got it correct. In general, this number, which is called the *difficulty index,* should range between .40 and .90 if the test items are to discriminate between the better and the poorer students. You may want to have a whole collection of 1.0 items (easy ones) to use at the beginning of your tests as positive start items.

Each time you perform an item analysis, record the date and the difficulty index on the back of the card where you keep your test items. This practice will enable you to improve your tests each time they are given. Test and item analyses are not one-shot practices—they should be done for each test and for each item each time it is used.

Item analysis serves as the basis for effective class discussion of tests. Item analysis helps the teacher clarify misconceptions, to determine when to reteach misunderstood subjects, and to learn why students have difficulty in interpreting some test items. Test and item analyses serve as a basis for general improvement in teaching while also helping to increase test construction skills.

SUMMARY

Writing test items is one thing; assembling, administering, and scoring tests is another. The process of assembling and administering a test begins with the creation of a table of test specifications and ends with an analysis of each item on the test. The table of test specifications will assist the teacher in determining whether all appropriate course objectives are included in the test and whether the items chosen are the best type to use to test for the performance called for in the objective. Some form of item bank, such as a card file or a computer file of test items, should be established and maintained for ease of test construction. The test should be constructed several days in advance of the time it is to be administered to allow for an unhurried appraisal of its quality.

Tests should be administered under the best possible physical and emotional conditions if the results are to be reliable. Unless the teacher has an inordinate amount of time to flip pages, some form of separate answer sheet should be provided for the students. Once a test has been administered and corrected, the teacher's work is still not complete, for all items should be analyzed to determine their validity and to improve them for the next administration.

DISCUSSION QUESTIONS

1. Do you think that test results should be the major basis upon which course grades are assigned? Why, or why not?

2. What is wrong with just using examinations (or quizzes, or daily assignments, or projects) to determine final course grades?

3. If all students get an item correct on a test, should the item be left out of future tests? Why?

4. When does an item discriminate positively?

EXERCISES

1. Perform a test and item analysis for an examination given in your class. Use all procedures outlined in this chapter.

2. Following is an exercise to put it all together. The purpose of this assignment is to put

into practice all that you have learned regarding item and test construction for the cognitive domain by constructing a comprehensive examination for at least one unit of instruction. This examination can be constructed from the items that you create for the weekly assignments.

A. Construct and duplicate an examination covering at least one unit of instruction.

B. Administer the examination to at least one class of your students.

C. Score all examinations, keeping appropriate records.

D. Perform an item analysis using the practices detailed in the text and class. Use an item analysis form such as one shown in the text, including a difficulty index.

E. Provide an interpretation of the items based on the item analysis. Analyze the response patterns where appropriate.

F. Turn in a copy of (1) the examination, (2) the record of scores omitting students' family names, (3) the completed item analysis forms, and (4) your interpretation of the item analysis with recommendations for changing or improving the test.

RESOURCES

A Reference List and Selected Bibliography

Brennan, R.L. (1972). A generalized upper-lower item discrimination index. *Educational and Psychological Measurement, 32,* 289–303.

Crehan, K.D. (1974). Item analysis for teacher-made mastery tests. *Journal of Educational Measurement, 2* (4), 255–262.

Lord, F.M. (1980). *Applications of item response theory to practical testing problems.* Hillsdale, NJ: Erlbaum.

Lyman, H.B. (1971). *Test scores and what they mean.* Englewood Cliffs, NJ: Prentice-Hall.

Traxler, A.E. (1951). Administering and scoring the objective test. In E.F. Lindquist (Ed.), *Educational measurement,* pp. 329–416. Washington, DC: American Council on Education.

Ward, W.C. (1984). Using microcomputers to administer tests. *Educational Measurement: Issues and Practice, 3* (2), 16–20.

▶ 13

Nontest Assessment Techniques

Early in this book it was stated that we all engage in evaluation activities every day. The same is true of classroom teachers—we all engage in evaluation of our students' progress every day, but we do not use formal tests every day to conduct the evaluation. Instead, we use in-class assignments, homework, group exercises, informal observation, critical observation, discussions with other teachers, and sometimes informed intuition just to assess the students' abilities to perform the skills that we have taught them. Educators have even taken a lesson from artists and models and now have students compile portfolios of their work in an attempt to measure ability and progress. Each of those techniques will be discussed in the following sections.

HOMEWORK

Homework is usually viewed as an instructional activity that has few if any implications for evaluation. It is not usually thought of as an assessment device, but it almost always plays a part in grading schemes (see Chapter 14). For example, homework is usually assigned with the purpose of providing a structured exercise that will help the student practice what has been taught. Sometimes teachers assign homework that deals with the theoretical aspects of the subject being taught and use class time to supervise and evaluate the more practical, hands-on work. One aspect of homework is that students should be able to—and do—get help with their homework, so the resulting product is not necessarily a good measure of their mastery of the subject. Teachers who rely too heavily on homework as part of an assessment strategy run the risk of creating students who become too concerned with getting the right answer at the expense of learning how or why to do something. In addition, student success on homework may be a better reflection of their ability to use other students and parents rather than of their actual mastery of the subject. In all cases, homework assignments should be well thought out and should relate to the objectives of the lesson and of the course. Homework just for the sake of doing homework produces assignments done just for the sake of doing assignments—nothing of consequence to the student or the teacher is really learned. Well-thought-out assignments that relate to course objectives can and should be used as part of a classroom assessment strategy.

CASE STUDIES AND PROBLEM-SOLVING ASSIGNMENTS

Case studies or problem solving exercises are other methods of instruction that may be used as evaluation or assessment techniques. Case studies require the students to use and apply knowledge, not just to recognize or recall information. With assignments of this type, students are required either to place themselves in or react to a situation in which their prior learning is needed to solve the problem or to evaluate the situation. In almost all cases, the performance assessed by application of case studies or problem solving exercises is performance of a high level in the domain. For example, the exercise statement could ask the student to make inferences or to extrapolate data. Students can be required to predict trends, to analyze situations or structures, or to judge the merits of ideas, methods, or solutions.

Case studies or problem-solving exercises are usually used to determine the extent of cognitive and affective domain learning, but with a little effort, manipulative performance can also be assessed. For example, if the objective called for students to be able to troubleshoot (analyze what is wrong) with a piece of equipment, a problem-solving assignment could be developed in which all the symptoms of the defective equipment were listed and the students would be required to describe the probable cause of the trouble. They could then be asked actually to repair the defective equipment using the skills and knowledge developed in the course.

Case studies or problem solving exercises should follow the same rules that apply to all assessment activities: They should be realistic and practical, they should be written at the level of comprehension of the students, they should require application of prior learning, and they should have instructions that clearly indicate to the students exactly what they are to do.

PROJECTS

Projects—at least from the students' perspectives—might better be termed "megaassignments." Projects are usually designed to require students to apply a great number of the skills they have developed in a course by producing a product of some kind. Project assignments are usually given early in the course of instruction and have a completion date some weeks or even months later. In most instances, projects are completed in class under the supervision of the teacher. This allows unhurried observation, often of the same kinds of performance, over an extended time. Teachers can get a reliable assessment of the abilities of the students under a variety of conditions and using the tools and equipment that they will use on the job.

Examples of projects might include a complete structure frame, for carpentry; a newsletter, for wordprocessing; an overhauled engine, for auto mechanics; or a small production, for television production. Projects might also be termed "extended tasks," or assignments that require sustained attention in a single work area carried out over hours or even days.

OBSERVATION

Certain aspects of student learning, such as the manner in which the students go about their daily activities, are best left to the considered judgment of the teacher. Observation of students for evaluation or assessment purposes involves much more than just watching them as they spend their day in the classroom. Instead, the observation of student behavior and performance and the subsequent recording of the results should follow an organized plan and be based on concrete, objective data. Observation should consider the students' efforts to perform the methods and procedures that have been demonstrated in class and to apply the information that has been presented, and should be done with the express purpose of evaluation in mind.

Well-done observation will allow the teacher to observe the students as they use and develop, on a daily basis, the skills taught. This has the secondary benefits of enabling the teacher to be aware of the results of the teaching effort, to detect and analyze learning difficulties, and to catch inappropriate skill patterns before they become ingrained.

Observation also provides an opportunity to evaluate learning outcomes without taking time from the instructional process for formal evaluation activities (tests). It also permits evaluation of behaviors that might not be easily observed in the confined situation of performance testing. Finally, observation facilitates the assessment of such behaviors as following safe practices, getting along with co-workers, taking directions "on the run," and caring for and maintaining tools and equipment (affective domain behaviors).

It is very important when using observation as an assessment tool—particularly when it will be used as part of a grade—to base the observation on the major objectives of the course and to have clearly in mind what is to be observed. Levels of proficiency should be specified (see Chapter 2) and students observed and evaluated accordingly. Other evaluation devices, such as written and performance tests, will often assist in determining behavior that should be observed by indicating areas where students are not performing adequately. Observations should be recorded on some form of progress chart (see Chapter 14) as they occur in order to have the most value.

If there are faults to using observation as an assessment tool, they come largely as a part of the judgmental nature of the activity. If the teacher has clearly in mind the course objectives and the standards of behavior, observation moves from the subjective to the objective realm. Teachers may have a tendency to let students' past performance influence their objectivity while observing, or to give high ratings to the students who appear to be busy all the time or who never cause trouble. As stated at the outset of this section, observation involves more than just watching the students. In addition to being as objective as possible, observation must be a deliberate act, not something hurriedly completed the day before grade reports are due.

PORTFOLIOS

Portfolios are collections of many projects that students have engaged in for significant periods of time and that have produced products. Portfolios represent the *best* work students have done. The clearest example of a portfolio that would be applicable to occupational education would be that of a photographer. In the same fashion that commercial photographers compile portfolios of their best work to demonstrate to prospective clients, photography students would compile portfolios of their best works to demonstrate their skills to prospective employers. For subjects that are paper-based, the compilation of a portfolio is a fairly simple matter. For subjects such as automechanics, carpentry, cosmetology, and other subjects that produce large items or require the use of tools and machinery, photographs, drawings, or videotapes may be used to illustrate progress. Teachers' anecdotal records of observations made during the process of creating the product illustrated may be included in the portfolio, either in writing or on audio- or videotape. Other teachers, parents, advisory group members, and school administrators can and should be used to review portfolios of student work and to make comments on the work.

In the absence of course objectives and other context information, it is often difficult for "outside" evaluators such as employers to determine what the student was supposed to do or be able to do. Outside evaluators are not aware of the time, resources, processes, or assistance students had in completing the work in the portfolio, so their evaluation will lack that perspective. Teachers, on the other hand, are in the best position to provide overall observations of the work illustrated in a portfolio. They have seen most of the work being accomplished and have observed the students in the development of the cognitive and manipulative skills necessary to complete the work.

ASSESSING AFFECTIVE BEHAVIOR

Assessing change or development in the affective domain is generally more difficult to accomplish reliably than in other domains. One technique that can be used to assess the achievement of affective domain objectives is the interview, either structured or unstructured. The structured interview is conducted one-on-one in private, and is carefully organized to insure that the students have the opportunity to express their attitudes and feelings on predetermined questions. Unstructured interviews are more like conversations with the students in which teachers brings up topics they want the students to talk about. In either case, the students should know the purpose of the interview, and it is a good idea to record them on audio- or videotape. Students are often assisted in expressing their feelings in unstructured interviews, but the teacher must be careful to not coach.

There are many types of attitude scales that can be developed to assess student achievement of affective domain objectives. Students can be asked to rate how strongly they feel about a particular topic, or they might be asked to rate two opposing words or ideas according to how they feel about them. Checklists of desired behavior may be created and either the teachers or the students themselves can check off the rate or degree of behavior achieved.

Practicing these and other techniques will help to provide reliable and accurate assessments of the development of behavior in the affective domain.

SHOE By Jeff MacNelly

Reprinted by permission: Tribune Media Services

SUMMARY

Just as written and performance test results cannot constitute an entire system of assessment of student performance, neither can assignments, portfolios, teacher observations, or projects. Instead, a more likely system would include written tests, performance examinations, written products such as essays, group (team) assignments, portfolios, self-observations, and observations by teachers and other expert persons.

An assessment system that is fair to the students and that tests all the student accomplishments, abilities, and values that society and educators profess as important will by necessity look far different from those commonly found in classrooms. While such a system will not be easy (or cheap) to develop, the quality of such assessment will be high, it will be valid and reliable, and most important, it will be effective in improving student performance.

EXERCISES

1. Select a performance objective from your occupation that requires analysis, synthesis, or evaluation, and construct a case study or problem solving assignment. Provide an indication of how you would score or evaluate, the exercise.

RESOURCES

A Reference List and Selected Bibliography

McRobbie, J. (1992). *Using portfolios to assess student performance.* San Francisco, CA: Far West Laboratory.

Wiggins, G. (1993, November). Assessment: Authenticity, context, and validity. *Phi Delta Kappan, 75* (3), 200–214.

▶ 14

Assigning Grades

This chapter examines the practice and technique of assigning grades. One of the major reasons for the measurement of student achievement is to obtain data that might serve as a basis for the assignment of course grades and the reporting of progress. In assigning grades and reporting achievement, some type of descriptive report often serves either as a substitute for or a supplement to the letter grade. Most teachers at all educational levels also must distribute As, Bs, Cs, Ds, and Fs to their students as marks that represent the students' levels of achievement in the courses or subjects.

GRADING SYSTEMS

Most schools use letter grades that are based on some percentage of 100. For example, 89.5 to 100 is often considered an "A," 79.5 to 89.5 a "B," and so on down. It is a simple matter to define what that scale is and to convert raw test scores to a percentage and assign grades accordingly. Schools and colleges convert the given letter grades to a grade point system. Such systems are then used to calculate overall grade point averages (GPA), which in turn are used to determine eligibility for certification, advancement, and future education. Some schools use a straight four-point system, while others use plus and minus grades. Examples of both systems follow.

Grades in the typical four point system are weighted as follows:

A = 4 points per unit
B = 3 points per unit
C = 2 points per unit
D = 1 point per unit
F = 0 points per unit

If, under this system, a student took four three-unit courses in one term and received an A, two Bs, and one C, the grade point average would be 4 + 3 + 3 + 2 = 12/4 = 3.0.

The plus and minus system provides different weights for the plus and minus grades as follows.

Grade	Description	Grade Points
A	Outstanding	4.0
A–		3.7
B+		3.3
B	Very Good	3.0
B–		2.7
C+		2.3
C	Average	2.0
C–		1.7
D+		1.3
D	Barely Passing	1.0
D–		0.7
F	Failure	0.0

The plus and minus system will provide a more accurate and reliable description of an individual's achievement level than will the straight four-point system.

Some teachers do not attempt to assign letter grades until the results of all graded activities are accumulated for a given grading period. If letter grades are to be assigned at the end of a given interval or at the end of the semester, they should also be assigned for each major test given and for each major project in order that students may be aware of their achievements and understand where they stand.

COMPONENTS OF GRADES

The basis for measuring achievement and for assigning grades should be a composite of various course activities and other factors. Specific values should be established for assignments, projects, quizzes, lengthy examinations, and other factors on which the students are evaluated, such as cooperation, attitudes demonstrated, and class participation. The evaluation system should be all-encompassing and should be based upon a composite of various course activities.

One system that is fairly objective is the point system. In the point system, the teacher establishes point values for each course activity and the students' final grades depend on the total points they earn throughout the course. An example of how such a system could be applied is as follows:

Attendance and class participation	100 points
Daily assignments	300 points
Quizzes	100 points
Midterm examination	100 points
Term project	200 points
Final examination	200 points
Total for course	1000 points

This example could be applied to any course wherein every activity can be given a definite point value and the students' efforts in each activity can be objectively graded. The total points accumulated can then be used to determine the final grade on a percentage basis. One problem with this system is that there is a tendency to place too much weight on midterm and final examinations. Another problem is that the system is rigid. All activities have to be planned well in advance of the course, and there is little or no room for spontaneous assignments or quizzes. This latter problem can be remedied by assigning percentages to the same activities.

"Do you handle report card work?"

FRED H. THOMAS 1994

The activities shown in the previous example would then be as follows:

Attendance and class participation	10%
Daily assignments	30%
Quizzes	10%
Midterm examination	10%
Term project	20%
Final examination	20%
	___
Total percentage	100%

Using a percentage system such as this will allow any number of daily assignments, each of which can have point values that vary depending on what the assignment is and the evaluative criteria used. Quizzes can be 8, 10, 17, or 28 points—whatever it takes to cover the topic. The same is true for major examinations: Specific numbers of items will not have to be included just to fit a point scheme. At the end of the course, each student's total points for assignments are added up and divided by the total points that were possible for assignments. The resulting number (a decimal) is multiplied by the percentage set for assignments at the beginning of the term. This number is the *percentage received* for assignments. The procedure is then repeated for quizzes, projects, and so on. Finally, all the percentages are added to get the final percentage, which is then converted to a letter grade using predetermined scales. (See Figure 14–1.)

ITEM	PTS. POSS.	PTS. REC'D	% POSS,	%REC'D
Attendance & Participation	15		15	
Daily Assignments	760		25	
Quizzes	176		20	
Midterm	100		10	
Project	200		15	
Final Exam	100		15	
			TOTAL	_____
			GRADE	_____

FIGURE 14–1 **Evaluation Criteria Form**

In many cases, it is not easy to justify the allocation when final course grades are calculated. In considering whether some adjustment should be made in the allocation of grades, the teacher should consider the following:

1. Within the distribution that was obtained, are there any natural groupings or clusters of scores? Since most of the measuring devices that we invent for classroom use are not accurate to within one point, the teacher might be hesitant, and rightly so, about including in the B category, for example, a score that is only one point above the highest score in the C group.

2. Is the class in question a normal group, or is it unusually high or low in abilities and accomplishments? If the class is unusually capable and great numbers of the students meet and exceed the evaluation criteria, the teacher might justify the assignment of As to a disproportionate percentage of the students. Many teachers assume, however, that their classes are superior and attempt to justify the assignment of higher grades than the situation warrants.

3. Note the mean scores. One way of determining the relative standing of the group in question is to compare the mean scores made by its members on specific tests or assignments with the mean scores made by other groups who have taken the same tests, that is, previous classes in the same subject. This will give you an idea of how the current class is performing relative to the previous classes and give you an idea of whether the evaluation criteria are still appropriate. What is the range of the scores for the current class? What is the mean score? How are the scores grouped around the mean? If the range of scores is very small, it will be difficult to justify assigning a wide range of grades.

For the final determination, it is necessary to inspect the obtained distribution and to consider all known facts about the students and about the nature of the subject that should have a bearing upon their grades. This will usually result in a revision of the obtained grade distribution.

If it can be assumed that the class to be assigned grades is a typical class, or if the school grading policy dictates that each student is to be marked in terms of the achievement of a particular class, the grades can be readily assigned by computing the mean and standard deviation without making significant adjustments. If, however, the distribution varies drastically, or if the class is considerably above or below average and must be compared with other classes in the school, drastic adjustments may be necessary. If grading must be done in terms of the achievement of a "normal" class, the mean of the scores made by such a class should be taken as the starting point for determining letter grades for a new class being tested. Fortunately, this is not a common occurrence.

THE "CURVE"

Teachers often remark that they grade "on the curve," and students, especially those who are concerned about how they are doing in a class, will ask if the teacher grades on the curve. The terminology originates from the so-called normal curve, or bell-shaped distribution (see Figure 14–2). The normal distribution is neatly divided into

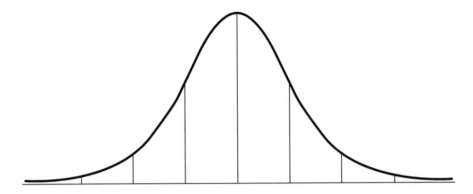

FIGURE 14–2 **The Normal Distribution, or Normal Curve**

six sections, three above the mean and three below. The two sections (called deviations)—the one directly above and the one directly below the mean—together constitute slightly more than two-thirds of the population represented. In a grading system truly based on the curve, the scores that fall in those two deviations together constitute the C grades for the test or course. The second deviation above the mean (13.3 percent) constitutes the B grades, while the same deviation below the mean constitutes the D grades. The A and F grades are those precious few that fall in the two tail areas of the distribution. Few students would want to be graded based on such a system, and few teachers would survive teaching more than a semester or so if they tried it!

Obviously, when people speak of grading on the curve, what they really mean is adjusting the scores and cutoff points to the abilities of the highest scoring students. This is a fine practice so long as the top-scoring students really tried hard and performed to the best of their ability, an assumption that most teachers are unwilling to make. A better practice is to determine the standards needed for success in the subject, set those same standards for performance in the classroom, and then adhere to them. If students consistently fail to meet the standards (come in low on the curve), then the standards and the teaching practices need to be examined. Perhaps the standards are too high for the groups of students being taught. Maybe the materials and equipment provided are not adequate. It could be that the teaching practices are not appropriate for the group or the subject.

In all cases, teachers must be as objective as possible in their grading and must not be influenced by factors that are not pertinent to the students' achievement. Teachers must be prepared to defend any grade they give. Developing a standard system of grading and then sticking to it will serve to increase objectivity and fairness and provide teachers with a firm basis for their grades. It will also go a long way to relieving the doubt that always comes with the assignment of grades.

DISCUSSION QUESTIONS

1. What are the arguments for and against the practice of using such factors as attendance, participation, interest, and attitude as part of a course grade?

2. What should teachers do periodically during a course to ensure that all students are aware of their progress?

3. Describe some situations where it would be appropriate for students to appraise their own progress, and situations where it would be appropriate to appraise each other's progress.

EXERCISES

1. On the basis of the materials presented in the text, in class, and on the assignments and activities unique to the course and the subject you teach, create a grading scheme that could be used to fairly determine grades in your teaching situation. You may use a point, percentage, or other scheme as appropriate, but include the following:

A. The title of the course and the educational level

B. The length of the course in hours (or appropriate units)

C. A statement or statements of the major course objectives in performance terms

D. Weights (in points if possible) and numbers of: (1) attendance and class participation, (2) daily assignments (what are they?), (3) quizzes, (4) large examinations, (5) projects, and (6) performance assessments

E. The portion (percentage) of the final grade determined by the elements in item C above

F. The scale used for assigning final grades

G. A sample of how you will communicate these requirements to your students (the syllabus distributed at the beginning of the course)

RESOURCES

A Reference List and Selected Bibliography

Ebel, R.L., & Frisbie, D.A. (1986). *Measuring educational achievement.* (Fourth edition). Englewood Cliffs, NJ: Prentice-Hall.

Pinchak, B.M., & Breland, H.M. (1974). Grading practices in American high schools: National longitudinal study of high school class of 1972. *Educational Digest, 39*, 21–23.

Terwilliger, J.S. (1971). *Assigning grades to students.* Glenview, IL: Scott, Foresman.

▶ 15

Evaluating
Instruction

Previous chapters presented various kinds of test items and other assessments that may be used as measuring instruments. Dozens of suggestions for constructing tests and many illustrations of good and poor testing practices were explored. If all of these efforts have been successful, your teaching will have become more effective.

It must be reiterated, however, that tests are not ends in themselves. They have little value unless the results are used to improve the teaching and learning that takes place. This means that you must study the results of all the assessments that you give and use them to bring about better student growth. Make assessment results a basis for improving your instruction. Be critical of your teaching efforts, but don't stop there. Periodically, ask questions such as the following:

1. Who is achieving as well as I had hoped?
2. In what ways can they be encouraged to make even greater progress?
3. Who is having trouble?
4. Where are they having trouble?
5. Why are they having trouble?
6. What method(s) of teaching can I use that might aid in improvement?
7. How can these method(s) best be carried out?

Review these questions after every test and assignment given to your students. Perhaps you will think of others that are even more helpful. The important point is that if such questions are answered, they will guide your thinking in working toward improved teaching.

Tests results will not supply all the answers to all these questions. Instead, it may be necessary to consult other sources such as the student's cumulative-record folder, data from the counselors, and grades in other courses. But a study of your own assessment results can start you on the way in a systematic, organized manner.

All evaluation efforts should be systematic and continuous. The biggest mistake teachers make is to consider evaluation as something to be tacked onto the instructional process around report-card time and then forgotten. Most teachers know this, but because of the time demands of teaching, many continue this casual practice.

One way around this weakness is to plan testing at the same time teaching is planned, such as was discussed in the Chapter 1. Testing, or assessment, then becomes an integral part of the teaching process. Knowing what you want to measure will be an invaluable help in knowing what and how to teach. An assessment program truly must be closely related to the objectives you are striving to achieve. In other words, while the objectives are being written, you should also be asking yourself how their attainment will be measured. This will not only help instructional activities and testing to be more effective, but will also help put meaning into the objectives.

Knowing the precise characterization of the changes sought in the students' behavior will also help you develop assessment activities that measure application, insight, and understanding of concepts and materials learned. It will be a useful means of keeping the measuring instruments practical and realistic rather than academic and farfetched. These thoughts are among the most important to carry with you in your teaching efforts.

It bears repeating that pencil-and-paper tests cannot do the whole job. Observation is probably one of the most important evaluating tools a teacher can use. Teachers observe every day, so it is important to make the process as objective as possible by knowing what is being observed and why. The simplest possible means for recording observations should be developed. In a sense, all tests should be tests of performance, but generally manipulative performance tests will be developed as instruments for measuring the attainment of manipulative skills. Like all tests, they demand careful organization and development.

Whatever the type of device used for testing, it should be constructed in terms of the two basic questions that have been repeated again and again: Exactly what is to be measured? How can it best be measured? When you know exactly what it is that is to be measured, it will be much easier to develop an instrument that is valid, reliable, objective, discriminating, comprehensive, and easy to administer and score. These qualities are the marks of a good test and should characterize all evaluation efforts.

Evaluation of students is based on reflective judgment, using all the pertinent data that can be gathered. Tests and testing are only a means to an end, and are useful only insofar as they bring about better teaching and learning. One of the primary means of obtaining data for reflective judgment is through the use of instructional evaluation, a process whereby the teacher has students and peers participate in the evaluation of instructional delivery. The ultimate purpose of the evaluation of instruction is to improve of the effectiveness of teachers. Through self-evaluation, evaluation by the students, and evaluation by peers, teachers become more competent and more aware of and accountable for actions in the classroom.

"I'd like to overwhelm them with instructional excellence, but I'm not above winning through intimidation."

2/81

© MARTHA F. CAMPBELL

When evaluating instruction, three major areas must be examined. First, the effects of the instruction on the students is determined by the students themselves. Second, the teachers evaluate their own plan of teaching. Third, the actual performance of the teacher is evaluated by the teacher's peers. Previous chapters were concerned with evaluation of student performance; the remainder of this chapter is concerned with evaluation of teacher performance.

EFFECT OF INSTRUCTION

The effect of the instruction on students includes the interest students display, their response in class, their success in practical activities, and test results. In the long run, teacher effect on students can be determined by examining the students' success on their future jobs or in more advanced educational situations. This, of course, requires the use of follow-up studies after graduation.

Student evaluation of instruction has been a hotly debated subject for many years. Arguments presented from both sides are valid: Some of it is good, some of it is not so good. The fact remains, however, that if students are irritated with something a teacher does, or clearly do not understand what is being done in class, then the teaching is not effective. In most cases, students are not competent to judge the quality of the technical material being presented to them, but they are competent to judge (or at least to comment on) the effectiveness of the manner in which it was presented. This is not a place for a complete discussion of student evaluation of instruction, but generally, students are able to comment on such things as the use of productive teaching techniques, the teacher's interpersonal relations skills, the organization of the presentations, and the classroom environment.

Several sample forms for student evaluation of instruction may be found in Appendix C, and sources for others appear in the bibliography at the end of this chapter. Chose an instrument, or adapt one for your use, and periodically administer it in your classes. Keep the evaluations anonymous so that students will feel free to respond openly. Tabulate the results and take them to heart. Then make a concerted effort to improve the areas in which the students feel you need improvement.

EVALUATION OF TEACHING PLANS

The evaluation of teaching plans includes the materials used in instruction, such as lesson plans, procedure sheets, instructional aids, texts and references, and other tangible items. The lesson and course objectives that are generated as a result of job, task, or content analysis should also be evaluated to determine whether they conform to standard practice.

Self-evaluation is something nearly everyone does all the time. It is a necessary adjunct to self-direction and personal discipline, both of which are characteristics that contribute to success on the job. Good teachers (who are also good mathematicians or welders or nurses or mechanics or from any number of other professions) always try to find ways to improve their effectiveness. One way to do this is to review every lesson as soon as possible after it has been taught to determine what was done well and what could have been improved. Mark comments and observations directly on the instructor's lesson plan so that they may be implemented the next time the lesson is taught. The Lesson Observation Rating Form found in Appendix C is one way of rating yourself, although it was designed to be used by others, particularly by peers. Another form of self-evaluation is personally to appraise whether you possess or demonstrate the traits that good teachers are "supposed" to have. Forms for doing just that may be found in several of the sources listed in the resource sections. Remember that self-evaluation is worthless without honesty and objectivity.

EVALUATION OF TEACHER PERFORMANCE

An evaluation of teacher performance is concerned with the delivery of instruction and its subsequent follow-through. Such characteristics as clear communication, eye contact, student involvement, technical accuracy, and use of the language are examined for their effect.

Experienced teachers and administrators are usually happy to assist new teachers by observing classes and commenting on technique and procedures used. When peer evaluation is voluntarily requested, the teacher being evaluated is under less stress and is less hesitant to discuss shortcomings. The forms in Appendix C provide a format based on the four-step instructional process, and they are easily adaptable to most teaching situations. Try using them yourself by visiting other teachers, with their permission, and observing their teaching. Share your observations with them if they ask, then have them reciprocate in your classes.

SUMMARY

The focus of this book has been on the development of assessment techniques for the students in learning situations. Assessment of student progress is one of the teacher's major responsibilities, but teachers also need to make yet one more assessment: that of their own abilities and performance in the classroom. Students, other teachers, and teachers themselves participate in this assessment. While students usually do not possess the technical skill to comment on the teacher's knowledge, they *are* in the best position to comment on the effect the instruction is having on their learning. Other teachers and administrators may be helpful in determining if the teaching plan, the materials developed, and the techniques of instruction used are the most appropriate and effective to use with the subject and the students in the class. When the evaluation of the teacher's effectiveness is added to the evaluation of the students' performance, the cycle of the instructional process depicted in Figure 1–1 is complete.

DISCUSSION QUESTIONS

1. Describe the major areas in which students are capable of evaluating their instructors.

2. Is it possible for students to comment accurately on the instructor's level of knowledge of the subject being taught?

3. What would you tell a new teacher who asked you for tips on how to make life as a teacher easier?

EXERCISES

1. Using one of the forms in Appendix C, have a supervisor observe you in the classroom and evaluate your instruction. Use the form that is most appropriate for the type of instruction you are delivering on the day you are observed—lecture or demonstration.

Discuss with the supervisor your strengths and weaknesses as determined by the form. Next, discuss with the supervisor the form itself and its applicability in your teaching situation. Then, revise the form to better fit your teaching situation. Justify the removal or addition of items or the changing of format.

2. Using the form or forms that you revised in exercise 1, have the students in at least one (but preferably more) of your classes evaluate your instruction. Tally all student responses and comments on the forms. Discuss the results of the evaluation by pointing out areas in which you are doing well and areas in which you are not doing so well. Indicate what you could do to improve your teaching.

RESOURCES

A Reference List and Selected Bibliography

Airasian, P.W. (1993, October). Teacher assessment: Some issues for principals. *NAASP Bulletin, 77*, 55–65.

Bloom, T.K. (1974). Peer evaluation: A strategy for student involvement. *Man/Society/Technology, 33* (5), 137–138.

Cohen, P.A. (1981). Student ratings of instruction and student achievement: A meta-analysis of multisection validity studies. *Review of Educational Research, 51*, 281–309.

Cranton, P.A., & Smith, R.A. (1986). A new look at the effect of course characteristics on student ratings of instruction. *American Educational Research Journal, 23*, 117–128.

Epstein, J.L. (1985). A question of merit: Principals' and parents' evaluations of teachers. *Educational Researcher, 14*, 3–10.

Gronlund, N.E. (1981). *Measurement and evaluation in teaching*. New York: Macmillan.

Smith, P.L. (1979). The generalizability of student ratings of courses: Asking the right questions. *Journal of Educational Measurement, 16*, 77–88.

APPENDIX A

Performance Examination

PERFORMANCE EXAMINATION

RETRIEVING A FILE FROM A DISK

NAME _____ DATE_____

All equipment and disks will be provided.
Materials needed:

1. IBM PC computer
2. Disk
3. Printer
4. Monitor
5. Keyboard
6. WordPerfect Program

Student Instructions

This performance test is designed to measure your skills in operating the IBM PC
and compatible computers using the WordPerfect Program.

Using the information provided, you will retrieve a file from disk, edit, print,
and save the document, and then exit the program.

Using the attached paragraph:

1. While in WordPerfect and with a clear screen, use the <Retrieve> command to
bring the Braham document onto the screen.
2. Using the command to move the cursor, and the Backspace and Del keys to
delete text, make the changes indicated in the Braham document.
3. Use the block delete operation to remove the third paragraph, beginning with the
words "You might also." If too many blank lines remain after deleting, remove those
lines as well. To delete a blank line, move cursor to the blank line to be removed and
press the Del key.
4. Make the changes indicated to the last paragraph.
5. After you have proofread your work, print the entire document.
6. Save the letter using the <Exit> command and then leave the WordPerfect program. Remember after making changes to a document that already exists on a disk,
you want to "Replace" the file, if asked.

BRAHAM DOCUMENT

I would like to apply for the Administrative position that you advertised in the Sunday <u>Tribune</u> newspaper.

As you will see in my attached resume, I am well qualified for this position. I will be graduating from (key your school's name here) in just a few months, and have extensive experience with WordPerfect and personal computers. I also enjoy travel, and feel it would be exciting to work in that industry.

You might also be interested to know that I am very active in school, work, and community activities. I am a part-time tutor in wordprocessing, a volunteer at a local nursing home, and a member of my school's student advisory council.

If you need any additional information or would like to schedule an interview, please feel free to call me at (key your phone number here). I look forward to hearing from you.

Skills to Be Evaluated

1. Use of function keys (Shifts - F3, F10)
2. Use of command keys (Backspace, Delete, and Replace)
3. Use of the menu
4. Removing extra lines from the document
5. Making changes in the paragraph
6. Printing the document

Standard

1. Use block style format.
2. Margin settings are 1.5" top, bottom, left, and right.
3. Double space between paragraphs.
4. Make sure all words are spelled correctly.
5. Show current date, your address.
6. Place information in the paragraphs indicated by the corrections.
7. Use mixed punctuation.
8. Use proper greetings (complimentary) and closings (salutation).

PERFORMANCE TEST RATING TEST

Student's Name _____   Date _____

Rated by   _____   Score _____

RATING SCALE

	Possible Points	*Given*
1. Used the correct greetings and closings	10	
2. Applied the current date	10	
3. Used the block style format	10	
4. Used mixed punctuation and double spaced	10	
5. Made necessary corrections	10	
6. Used the function keys to save and print	10	
7. Used the command keys to delete, backspace, and replace	20	
8. Proofread document and correct margins	10	
9. Saved the document on the disk	10	
Total points	100	

Item Analysis Forms

ITEM ANALYSIS CALCULATION SHEET

ITEM	NUMBER CORRECT HIGH	LOW	H+L	H+L/N	DIFFICULTY	ANALYSIS

ITEM #	T A	F B	C	D	E	NUMBER WRONG	NUMBER RIGHT

▶ APPENDIX C

Instructional
Evaluation Forms

LESSON OBSERVATION RATING FORM

Name of Person Giving Lesson_____

Location_____

Date   _____   Time _____

Class Level (Grade)   _____

Number of Students   _____

Title of the Lesson   _____

Instructions

The purpose of this rating scale, which is based on the four-step instructional system, is to create a consciousness on your part of the vital points that seriously affect the success of a teacher. Ratings are of value only if they are made with complete frankness. You may wish to clarify some of the ratings by making comments in the space provided. A rating of "4" would be very good, or high, while a rating of "1" would be poor.

Motivation

(Step 1) Time spent _____ minutes.   4   3   2   1   N/A

1. How well did the teacher "prepare" the
   class?
2. Did the teacher find out what the students
   knew about the lesson?

Presentation

(Step 2) Time spent _____ minutes.

3. Were trade terms and technical words
   explained?
4. How well was the lesson held to the
   topic?
5. Were practical examples used to clarify
   points in the lesson?

	4	3	2	1	N/A

6. Did the teacher refrain from "talking to the board"?

7. Was the chalkboard work clear?

8. Did the teacher look at ALL students?

9. Were the visual aids used effectively?

10. Was the lesson summarized?

11. Overall quality of the demonstration, experiment, or lecture was

Application

(Step 3) Time spent _____ minutes.

12. Was the teacher successful in keeping the discussion related to the subject?
13. Did the teacher maintain the interest of the class?
14. Did the teacher stimulate student participation in the lesson?
15. Was there a frequent check-up for understanding of the things taught?

16. Were the questions clear?

17. Were good questioning techniques used?

Evaluation

(Step 4) Time spent _____ minutes.

18. How well was the lesson summarized and student understanding checked?

19. Quality of the testing?

Personality Traits

20. Voice quality

21. Enthusiasm

22. Posture

	4	3	2	1	N/A
23. Mannerisms					
24. Use of English					
25. Appropriate Dress					
26. "Professionalism"					

Preparation by the Teacher

27. Did the lesson appear to be well-planned?

28. Were all charts, tools, tests, films, instruction sheets, and other aids ready for use?

29. Your overall rating of the lesson

30. How would you characterize the mode of instruction used in this lesson (if more than one applies, check all)?

_____ Lecture   _____ Multi-media oriented
_____ Demonstration   _____ Resource speaker
_____ Discussion   _____ Role playing
_____ Small groups   _____ Other
_____ Supervised study

Comments:

LECTURE ANALYSIS

		POINTS POSSIBLE	POINTS RECEIVED
STUDENT INSTRUCTOR	**STUDENT OBSERVER**		
LESSON TITLE	**DATE**		
NOTE: Observers should give careful analysis to the following items. Make specific remarks and suggestions, not comments such as "good," "fair," or "poor."			
ITEM **ANALYSIS**			
APPEARANCE & SELF CONFIDENCE		10	
ENTHUSIASM & BODY VITALITY		10	
CONTACT WITH CLASS Eye contact Level of language		10	
VOICE VARIETY & SPEECH Rate and tone Absence of mannerisms		10	
INTRODUCTION Review Tie-back Value Arouse interest Objectives		10	
LOGICAL DEVELOPMENT Sequence Time Transitions		10	
EXPLANATIONS Clarity Examples Level		10	
TRAINING AIDS Selection Use		10	
CHECKED STUDENT UNDERSTANDING Periodic check Questions & comments period		10	
SUMMARY Recap main points & tie-in Conclusions reached		10	

TOTAL POINTS 100

TEACHER PERFORMANCE ASSESSMENT FORM

DEMONSTRATE A MANIPULATIVE SKILL

Name _____ Date _____

Resource Person _____

Directions: Indicate the level of the teacher's accomplishment by marking the appropriate box under the LEVEL OF PERFORMANCE heading. If, because of special circumstances, a performance component was not applicable, or impossible to execute, mark the N/A box.

LEVEL OF PERFORMANCE

	N/A	None	Poor	Fair	Good	Excellent
1. The physical environment was reasonably comfortable	☐	☐	☐	☐	☐	☐
2. The physical setting for the demonstration was as close to actual conditions on the job as possible	☐	☐	☐	☐	☐	☐
3. All necessary tools, materials, supplies, and visuals were organized and at hand when the teacher needed them	☐	☐	☐	☐	☐	☐
4. All tools, materials, supplies, and visuals were in good condition	☐	☐	☐	☐	☐	☐
5. The teacher introduced the demonstration with explanations of:	☐	☐	☐	☐	☐	☐
a. what was going to be demonstrated	☐	☐	☐	☐	☐	☐
b. how it fit in with what the class already knew or had experienced	☐	☐	☐	☐	☐	☐
c. how it fit in with future activities	☐	☐	☐	☐	☐	☐
6. The teacher defined any new terms that would be encountered during the demonstration	☐	☐	☐	☐	☐	☐

	N/A	None	Poor	Fair	Good	Excellent
7. The teacher motivated the class to want to learn the new skill	☐	☐	☐	☐	☐	☐
8. Each step necessary to the operation was demonstrated	☐	☐	☐	☐	☐	☐
9. Each step was explained as it was demonstrated	☐	☐	☐	☐	☐	☐
10. The steps were presented in a logical order	☐	☐	☐	☐	☐	☐
11. Key points or specific techniques essential to performing each step were explained	☐	☐	☐	☐	☐	☐
12. Safety practices specific to the operation were covered	☐	☐	☐	☐	☐	☐
13. If a step involved very small parts or intricate processes, the teacher used visuals or models to clarify the step	☐	☐	☐	☐	☐	☐
14. If a step was normally time-consuming (i.e., "clamp for three hours"), the teacher had completed the step ahead of time	☐	☐	☐	☐	☐	☐
15. The procedure followed for the operation was the one most commonly used in the field	☐	☐	☐	☐	☐	☐
16. The steps were presented slowly enough that students did not miss key points	☐	☐	☐	☐	☐	☐
17. Every movement in the demonstration was clearly visible	☐	☐	☐	☐	☐	☐
18. If direction of movement was of special importance, students were positioned accordingly	☐	☐	☐	☐	☐	☐
19. The teacher could be clearly heard	☐	☐	☐	☐	☐	☐
20. The teacher talked to the students, and not to the materials	☐	☐	☐	☐	☐	☐
21. The teacher performed the operation with ease	☐	☐	☐	☐	☐	☐

	N/A	None	Poor	Fair	Good	Excellent
22. The teacher set up standards of workmanship by doing a good thorough job	☐	☐	☐	☐	☐	☐
23. The teacher encouraged questions	☐	☐	☐	☐	☐	☐
24. The teacher asked key questions throughout to ensure that the students understood the demonstration	☐	☐	☐	☐	☐	☐
25. The teacher included some activity to summarize the steps and key points	☐	☐	☐	☐	☐	☐
26. The scope of the demonstration was sufficiently limited that students could absorb it all	☐	☐	☐	☐	☐	☐

<u>Level of Performance:</u> All items must receive N/A, GOOD, or EXCELLENT responses. If any item receives a NONE, POOR, or FAIR response, the teacher and resource person should meet to determine what additional activities the teacher needs to complete in order to reach competency in the weak area(s).

Comments:

Index